RICH DAD'S
GUIDE TO
BECOMING RICH

WITHOUT CUTTING UP
YOUR CREDIT CARDS

Turn Bad Debt Into Good Debt

ROBERT T. KIYOSAKI

RICH DAD'S
GUIDE TO
BECOMING RICH

WITHOUT CUTTING UP
YOUR CREDIT CARDS

Turn Bad Debt Into Good Debt

ROBERT T. KIYOSAKI

PLATA
PUBLISHING

Published by Plata Publishing, LLC

CASHFLOW, Rich Dad, Rich Dad Advisors, ESBI, and B-I Triangle are registered trademarks of CASHFLOW Technologies, Inc.

    are registered trademarks of CASHFLOW Technologies, Inc.

Plata Publishing, LLC
4330 N. Civic Center Plaza
Suite 100
Scottsdale, AZ 85251
(480) 998-6971
Visit our websites: PlataPublishing.com and RichDad.com

Printed in the United States of America
First Edition: 1998
First Plata Publishing Edition: 2011
ISBN: 978-1-61268-035-4

Cover photo credit: Seymour & Brody Studio

BEST-SELLING BOOKS

BY ROBERT T. KIYOSAKI

Rich Dad Poor Dad
What the Rich Teach Their Kids About Money—
That the Poor and Middle Class Do Not

Rich Dad's CASHFLOW Quadrant
Guide to Financial Freedom

Rich Dad's Guide to Investing
What the Rich Invest in That the Poor and Middle Class Do Not

Rich Dad's Rich Kid Smart Kid
Give Your Child a Financial Head Start

Rich Dad's Retire Young Retire Rich
How to Get Rich Quickly and Stay Rich Forever

Rich Dad's Prophecy
Why the Biggest Stock Market Crash in History Is Still Coming...
And How You Can Prepare Yourself and Profit from It!

Rich Dad's Success Stories
Real-Life Success Stories from Real-Life People
Who Followed the Rich Dad Lessons

Rich Dad's Guide to Becoming Rich
Without Cutting Up Your Credit Cards
Turn Bad Debt Into Good Debt

Rich Dad's Who Took My Money?
Why Slow Investors Lose and Fast Money Wins!

Rich Dad Poor Dad for Teens
The Secrets About Money—That You Don't Learn In School!

Rich Dad's Escape from the Rat Race
How to Become a Rich Kid by Following Rich Dad's Advice

Rich Dad's Before You Quit Your Job
Ten Real-Life Lessons Every Entrepreneur Should Know
About Building a Multi-Million-Dollar Business

Rich Dad's Increase Your Financial IQ
Get Smarter with Your Money

Conspiracy of the Rich
The 8 New Rules of Money

CONTENTS

INTRODUCTION

Most people are familiar with the television show, *Who Wants to Be a Millionaire?* It was an overnight success in the United States and was soon viewed by audiences around the world. All the contestants had to do was answer a series of trivia questions. With each correct response, they earned more cash, culminating with a possible jackpot of $1 million.

It wasn't long before the question, "Who wants to be a millionaire?" became a popular catchphrase everywhere. With so much fixation on money, getting rich, and huge lottery payouts, the more obvious question is: "Who *doesn't* want to be a millionaire?"

And yes, it is possible to win a million dollars on a game show. It is also possible to get millions of dollars by winning the lottery. And it is possible to become a millionaire by investing in an IPO (initial public offering). Then you could retire rich for the rest of your life. In fact, there are more ways to become rich today than in any other time in our history. Maybe that is why there is such an international frenzy over the idea of getting rich—and the quicker the better.

I remember when I was being interviewed about my book, *Rich Dad Poor Dad*, and the interviewer asked, "Come on, why don't you tell us the truth? Didn't you write your book simply to take advantage of this get-rich-quick craze that is sweeping the nation?"

Her question really surprised me, and I was almost at a loss for words. I finally replied, "You know, I never saw it that way. And I can see why you would think I would write a book just for that reason. I wish I could say I was that smart—smart enough to time my book for just this moment in history—but I'm afraid I'm not. I wrote this book because I wanted to tell the story of the money lessons I learned from my two dads."

I paused and said, "My book actually represents the exact opposite message of these game shows and lotteries. There is indeed a frenzy today about getting rich quick. While my book is about getting rich, it is *not* about getting rich quick."

The commentator nodded and gave me a skeptical grin. "So if you are not part of this get-rich-quick mania, then what are you proposing? Get rich *slowly*?"

I could feel her sarcasm, and it challenged me. In front of millions of viewers I had to try to keep my cool. So I forced a chuckle in response to her barbed comment and said, "No, my book is not about getting rich quickly or getting rich slowly." I then smiled and waited for her to ask me the next question. The silence was deafening, but I held my ground as calmly as possible, waiting for her to make the next move.

She smiled and asked, "So what *is* your book about?"

I grinned and replied, "It's about the *price* of getting rich."

"The price?" she replied. "What do you mean by 'the price'?"

As she asked the question, the producer signaled to her that we were out of time. She then urged me to hurry with my answer, and I ended the interview by saying, "Most everyone wants to get rich. But the problem is that only a few people are willing to pay the price."

The TV interview was over. The host thanked me and they cut to the final commercial. I was never able to address what I think the price of becoming rich actually is. This book answers that question.

Who Pays the Price?

One government study tracked people from the ages of 20 to 65. By the time they turned 65 years old, the study found that:

1%	were wealthy
4%	were well off
5%	were still working because they had to
54%	were living on support from family or the government
36%	were dead

In addition, more than 35 percent of that wealthy 1 percent inherited their wealth, as did a large percentage of the 4 percent who were well off.

Yet the question remains: What did the top 5 percent of the rich do that the others did not? What price did the 5 percent pay that the others did not?

Does a Big House Mean You're Rich?

When I was young, my rich dad drove me past a classmate's house located in a very wealthy neighborhood. I asked rich dad if my classmate's dad was rich. Rich dad chuckled and responded, "A high-income job, a big house, nice cars, and lavish vacations do not mean you're rich. In fact, it could mean exactly the opposite. A lavish lifestyle does not mean you're smart or well educated. It could mean exactly the opposite."

Most of us are wise enough to understand what rich dad meant by that statement. Yet I think one of the reasons so many people faithfully play the lottery is because they, too, would like to have a nice big house, expensive cars, and all the other toys that money can buy. While it is possible to gain millions by winning the lottery, in reality, the chances of doing so are extremely slim. Just as a big house does not necessarily mean you're rich, sitting around watching a game show or betting on your lucky numbers is not the price that most of the top 1 percent paid to become rich.

What Is the Price to Become Rich?

There are many different ways to become rich. Winning the lottery or winning on a game show are just two examples. You can also become rich by being cheap, becoming a crook, or even marrying a wealthy person. Many people actively look for rich people to marry.

Be forewarned: With any method of attaining great wealth, there is a price, and the price is not always measured in money.

The price for watching game shows and betting on the lottery is that *the vast majority will never become rich—and that is a very steep price to pay.* There are better ways to become rich, with much better odds, but most people are not willing to pay the price. In fact, there are some ways of becoming rich in which the odds are in the person's favor, almost guaranteeing that a person will become rich, but again the problem is that most people are not willing to pay the price. And that is why, according to the study, only 1 percent actually become rich—in the richest country in the world. They want to be rich, but they are not willing to pay the price.

So what is the price? If I said, "I wish I had the body of a world-class athlete," most of you would tell me, "Put on your running shoes, run five miles a day, go to the gym for three hours a day, and stop stuffing your face with pizza." That is what I mean by the price.

And I would probably reply, "Is there another way to have a body like that?" Millions of people would like to have a great body, but few people are willing to pay the price. And that is why they fall for phoney money-making ads that promise, "You will lose weight and still be able to eat all you want. Just take this little magic pill." Or, "You can look like this gorgeous model without exercise or dieting." Regardless if it's money, a sexy body, great relationships, happiness, or whatever we as humans have a desire for, Madison Avenue will come up with an ad campaign that promises the quick and easy way to get what you want. However, most of the products the ads promote do not work, and the people who buy them are not willing to do the hard work themselves or pay the real price.

I often refer to the $385 real estate investment course I purchased from a television infomercial many years ago. I remember sitting at home surfing the channels when I came across this infomercial. The ad encouraged me to come to a free evening seminar at the Hilton Hawaiian Village, a hotel on Waikiki Beach right next to the condominium where I lived. I called to make my reservation and attended the free seminar. Then I signed up for the $385 weekend seminar. I was still in the Marine Corps at that time, so I invited a fellow Marine pilot to go with me to the weekend seminar. He hated the seminar, called it a complete rip-off, a waste of time, and asked for a refund. Back at the squadron, he said to me, "I knew it was going to be a rip-off. I should never have listened to you."

My experience was completely different. I left the seminar, took the books and tapes, read and listened to them, and have made millions of dollars from the information I learned at that seminar. As a friend of mine said to me a number of years later, "The problem with your friend was that he was too smart and did not get anything from the course. You were stupid enough to believe the instructor and went out and did what he taught you."

Today, I continue to recommend that people sign up for seminars to learn the basics of buying real estate, starting a business, investing in stocks, or whatever. I often hear back from the audience, "But what if the course is no good? What if I get ripped off? What if I don't learn anything? Besides, I don't want to fix toilets or have midnight phone calls from tenants." When I hear such comments, I usually reply, "Then it is best that you do not attend the seminar. The seminar will definitely be a rip-off."

In my experience, many people are looking for the answers that will make their lives better in some way. The problem is that, when they find the answer, they don't like it—just as I don't like the answer, "Stop stuffing your face with pizza, and start pumping iron for three hours day." In other words, until I like the answer I'm getting, I don't have a prayer of developing the body of a world-class athlete. The reason most people will never become rich is simply because they don't like the answers they are getting. And in my opinion, it's more than just the answer they don't like. It is the price attached to the answer that the person really doesn't like.

As rich dad said, "Most people want to get rich. They just don't want to pay the price."

In this book I discuss the price of becoming rich without being cheap, crooked, or needing to marry a rich person. But there is a price—and as my rich dad often said to me, "The price of something is not always measured in money." In this book I share, not only the answers, but the price I paid. If you don't like my answers or my rich dad's answers, remember that there is more than one way to become rich. There will always be a new lottery or game show that asks the question, "Who wants to be a millionaire?"

CHAPTER ONE

WHAT IS THE PRICE OF BEING CHEAP?

"Most people want to get rich.
They just don't want to pay the price."

– Rich dad

There are many books that popularize the idea of frugality and living below your means. Many so-called money experts write and speak about the virtues of cutting up your credit cards, saving money, putting the maximum amount into your retirement plan, driving a used car, living in a smaller house, clipping coupons, shopping at sales, eating at home, passing used clothes from older kids down to the younger kids, taking cheaper vacations, and other strategies.

While these are excellent ideas for many people, and while there is a time and place for frugality, most people do not like these ideas. They would love to enjoy the finer things of life. A big home, a new car, fun toys, and expensive vacations are much more fun and desirable than putting money away in a bank. Most of us tend to agree with the wise sages professing frugality and economic abstinence. Yet deep down, many of us would rather have a platinum credit card without a spending limit—one that is paid for by a rich uncle who has more money than all the Arab oil sheiks, private Swiss banks, and Bill Gates combined.

We realize that it is the unbridled desire for the fun, fine, and fancy things of life that gets many people in financial trouble. And it is the financial trouble that these desires spawn that causes the money gurus to say, "Cut up your credit cards. Live below your means. Buy a used car."

On the other hand, my rich dad never said to me, "Cut up your credit cards." He never said, "Live below your means." Why would he advise me to do things he personally did not believe in? When it came to the idea of frugality, he did say, "You can become rich by being cheap. But the problem is that, even though you're rich, you're still cheap. You're skimping and saving and cutting corners… always choosing the least costly options on everything from bottled water to hotel rooms." He would further say, "It makes no sense to me to live cheap and die rich. Why would anyone want to live cheap, die rich, and then have the kids spend your life's savings after the funeral?" Rich dad noticed that people who scrimped and saved all their lives often had children who acted like starving hyenas once the parents were gone. Instead of enjoying their parents' inheritance, they often fought over the money and spent it all soon after they got their hands on what they called their "fair share."

Instead of telling me to pinch pennies, rich dad often said, "If you want something, find out the price. Then pay the price." He also went on to say, "But always remember, everything has a price. And the price for becoming rich by being cheap is that you're still cheap."

The Different Ways You Can Become Rich

You can become rich by marrying someone for his or her money. I had a classmate in New York who often said, "It is just as easy to marry a rich girl as a poor girl." When he graduated, he married into a very rich family just as he said he would. I personally think he was a slimeball for doing that, but that was his way of becoming rich.

You can become rich by becoming a crook, and we all know the price of that choice. When I was a kid, I thought a crook wore a mask and robbed banks. Today, I realize that there are many crooks that wear blue suits, white shirts, red ties, and who are often respected members of their community.

There are others who become rich by betting at the casino or racetrack, by playing the lottery, or by blindly throwing their money into the stock market. During the dot-com mania, I knew many people who were ready to write a check if all you said was, "I'm starting an Internet company."

You can become rich by being a bully, and we all know what happens to a bully. Eventually, an even bigger bully comes along. Or the bully discovers that the only people willing to do business with him or her are people who enjoy being pushed around.

As described earlier, you can become rich by being cheap. The world tends to despise rich people who are cheap—people like Scrooge in Charles Dickens' classic, *A Christmas Carol*. Most of us have met people who always want a larger discount, complain about the bill, or even worse, refuse to pay the bill for one frivolous reason or another. A friend who owns a dress shop often complains about the type of customer who buys a dress, wears it to a party, and then returns it a few days later, asking for her money back. And of course, there are those who drive old cars, wear clothes too long, buy cheap shoes, and look poor, but have millions of dollars in the bank.

While these individuals can become rich by being cheap, there is a price far beyond money for such behavior. I personally struggle with being too cheap at times, and yet I notice that people tend to smile more or like me more when I am generous. For example, when I tip a little extra for good service, it comes back to me in other ways. In other words, people tend to like generous people more than cheap people.

Can Everyone Be Rich?

Rich dad and I talked further about the price of being rich. He told me, "The price is different for different people."

"What do you mean by 'the price is different for different people'?" I asked.

His reply was, "I like to think that we all come into this world with unique gifts and talents such as singing, painting, athletics, writing, parenting, preaching, teaching, and so on. Although God gives us these talents, it is up to each of us to develop those talents—and developing those talents is often the price we pay to be rich."

Rich dad continued, "The world is filled with smart, talented, and gifted people who are not what we would call successful financially, professionally, or in their personal relationships. While each of us has gifts and strengths, each of us also has personal challenges and weaknesses to overcome. No one is perfect. That is why I say that the price is different for different people—because each of us has different challenges. The only people who think life should be easy are lazy people."

I do not know if rich dad's statement about lazy people is true or not. I do know that his statement has been useful for me whenever I find myself complaining about things not being easy or things not going my way. When I find myself saying, "I wish things were easier," I know I am getting lazy. So I take a break, check my attitude, and ask myself about the long-term price of having that attitude. It's not that I don't look for an easier way to do things. I am simply aware that when I tend to be lazy, cheap, or act like a spoiled brat, I need to ask myself what the price might be for that behavior.

Money Is the Reward for Paying the Price

Rich dad would also say, "Ask anyone who is rich, famous, or successful, and I am sure they will tell you that they had and have personal challenges and demons to face every day along the way. There is no free lunch. My challenge was that I had no education and no money when I started out. I also had a family to feed when my father died. I was thirteen years old when I was given that challenge—and there were even greater challenges to come. Yet I managed to pay the price and, in the end, I achieved great wealth. In hindsight, money was my reward for paying the price."

The Price of Security

Over the years, rich dad made sure that his son Mike and I were always aware of the price of something. When my real dad, the man I call my poor dad, advised me to find "a safe secure job," rich dad's reply was, "Remember, there is a price for security."

When I asked him what the price was, he answered, "For most people, the price of security is personal freedom. And without freedom, many people spend their lives working for money, rather than living out their dreams. For me, to live life without achieving my dreams is much too high a price to pay for security."

He also commented on taxes, saying, "People who seek security over freedom pay more in taxes. That is why people who have safe, secure jobs pay more in taxes than people who own the businesses that provide the jobs."

I spent a few days thinking about that comment, letting the magnitude of the idea sink in. The next time I saw rich dad, I asked him, "Do I have to choose between security or freedom? In other words, does that mean I can have one, but not the other?"

Rich dad laughed after he realized how much thought I had given to his remark. "No," he replied, still chuckling. "You don't have to have one or the other. You can have both."

"You mean I can have both security and freedom?" I asked.

"Sure," he said. "I have both."

"So why did you say that, for most people, the price of security is personal freedom?" I asked. "How can you have both when you say most people can have only one? What's the difference?"

"The price," said rich dad. "I've always said to you that everything has a price. Most people are willing to pay the price for security, but they are not willing to pay the price for freedom. That is why most people have only one of the two. They only have one or the other."

"And why do you have both security and freedom?" Mike asked. He had just entered the room and had heard only part of the conversation.

"Because I paid twice the price," said rich dad. "I was willing to pay the price for both security and freedom. It's no different than having two cars. Let's say I need a truck, but I also want a sports car. If I want both, I pay twice the price. Most people go through life paying for one or the other, but not both."

"So there is a price for security, and there is a price for freedom," I said. "And you paid the price for both." I repeated what rich dad had just said so that I could let the idea sink into my head.

Rich dad nodded. "Yes, but let me add one more point to clarify what it means to be willing to pay the price to have both. You see, we all pay a price anyway. We pay a price even if we don't pay the price."

"What?" I replied, frowning and shaking my head. Rich dad now seemed to be speaking in circles.

"Let me explain," said rich dad, gesturing with his hands that we should calm down. "Do you remember when I helped the two of you with your science homework a few weeks ago when you were studying Newton's laws?"

Mike and I nodded.

"Do you remember the third law: *For every action, there is an equal and opposite reaction?*"

Again we nodded.

"That is kind of how a jet flies through the air," said Mike. "The engine propels hot air backward, and the jet moves forward."

"That's right," said rich dad. "Since Newton's laws are universal laws, they apply to everything, not only jet engines." Rich dad looked at the two of us to see if we were following what he had just said. "Everything," he repeated, just to make sure we understood.

"Okay, everything," said Mike, a little frustrated at the repetition.

Suspecting that we were not really getting his point about everything, rich dad continued, "When I say 'everything,' I mean it quite literally." He went on, "Do you recall my lessons about financial statements? Do you remember my explanation that, if there is an *expense*, then there must be *income* somewhere else?"

Now I was beginning to understand what he meant by "everything." Newton's universal laws also applied to financial statements.

"So for every *asset*, there has to be a *liability*," I said. Just to let him know that I was beginning to follow his thinking, I added, "A universal law applies to everything."

"And for something to be *up*, something else must be *down*. And for something to be *old*, something else has to be *new*," added Mike.

"Correct," rich dad said with a smile.

"So how does this apply to security and freedom and your willingness to pay twice the price?" asked Mike.

"Good question," said rich dad. "It's important because, if you don't pay twice the price, you'll never get what you want anyway. In other words, if you don't pay twice the price, you do not get what you paid for in the first place."

"What?" I replied. "If you don't pay twice, you don't get what you paid for?"

Rich dad nodded his head and began to explain. "People who pay the price only for security may never really feel secure—like in job security," he stated boldly. "A person may have a false sense of security, but they never really feel secure."

"So even though my dad has what he thinks is a safe, secure job, deep down he never really feels secure?" I asked.

"That's correct," said rich dad. "Because he is paying only for the action, but not for his internal reaction. The harder he works for security or pays the price for security, the more his insecurity grows inside him."

"Does insecurity have to be the reaction?" Mike asked.

"Good question," rich dad said. "No, there can be other kinds of reactions. A person could have so much security that the reaction is boredom and then restlessness. They want to move on, but they don't because then they would give up their security. So that is why I say that each of us has different challenges, and each of us is unique. We're unique because we don't react to things in the same ways that others do."

"Like some people see a snake and panic, and others see a snake and get happy," I added.

"That's correct. We are all different because we are all wired differently," rich dad said.

"So what is the point of all these mental gymnastics?" I asked.

"The gymnastics are to make you think," said rich dad. "I always want you to remember that everything has a price—and that the price is often twice as much as it seems. If you pay for only one side of Newton's law, you may think you have paid the price, but you may not get what you want."

"Can you give us some examples?" I asked.

"I can give you general ones because, as I said, each of us is unique," said rich dad. "But, as a general rule, always remember that there are two sides to each situation.

"For instance, the best employer has usually started his or her career as an employee. He or she uses that prior experience as an employee to develop a management style that empowers the employees he or she manages."

"So good employers will be honest and treat their employees like they would like to be treated?" I asked.

"Exactly," rich dad replied. "Now let's look at an extreme example. What do you think it takes to be a good detective?"

"To be a good detective?" Mike and I repeated in tandem, thinking that rich dad was now driving down the wrong side of the road.

"Yes, a good detective," rich dad continued. "To be a good detective, a detective must first be honest, moral, and of the highest integrity. Is that correct?"

"I would hope so," said Mike.

"But to be good, a detective must also think exactly like a crook or someone who is immoral, unlawful, and unethical," said rich dad. "Always remember Newton's law. You cannot be a good detective without also being able to think like a good crook."

Mike and I were now nodding. We were finally beginning to understand where rich dad was going with this whole lesson.

"So that is why a person who tries to become rich by being cheap still winds up, in many ways, as poor as someone who has no money?" I asked.

Rich dad continued, "And why someone who seeks *only* security never really feels secure. Or why someone who seeks low-risk investments never feels investing is safe, and why someone who is always right eventually winds up wrong. They pay the price for one side of the equation, but fail to pay the full price. They violate a universal law."

Mike chimed in, "That is why it takes two people to have a fight. And to be a good detective, you have to also be a good crook. To lower risk, you have to take risks. To be rich, you have to know what it is like to be poor. To know what a good investment is, you have to also know what a bad one is."

"And that is why most people say investing is risky," I added. "Most people think that, to invest in a safe investment, you must also lower your return on the investment. That is why so many people put money in a savings account. They put it in for security and are willing to take less interest for that safety. But their money is being eaten away by inflation. And the interest on their money is taxed at a high rate. So their safe-as-money-in-the-bank idea is not such a safe idea."

Rich dad concurred. "Having money in the bank is better than not having money in the bank. But you are correct by saying that it's not as safe as they may like to think. There is a price for that illusion of safety."

Mike then turned to his dad and said, "You've always said that it's possible to have low-risk investments with very high returns."

"Yes," replied rich dad. "It is relatively easy to have security and still get a 20 to 50 percent return without paying a lot in taxes or using much of your own money—if you know what you are doing."

"So what you're telling us now," Mike said, "is that the price you paid was higher than what the average investor is willing to pay."

Rich dad nodded. "Always remember that everything has a price, and that price is not always measured in money."

The Price of Being Cheap

When I hear money gurus say, "Cut up your credit cards, buy a used car, and live below your means," I know they mean well. But as my rich dad said, "Everything has a price." And the price for becoming rich by being cheap is that you still wind up being cheap. And living life as a rich but cheap person is, in my opinion, a very high price to pay.

Rich dad also said, "The problem is not the credit cards. It is the financial illiteracy of the person holding the credit cards that is the problem. Getting financially literate is part of the price you need to pay to become rich."

And that is why so many people do not like the idea of cutting up their credit cards and living below their means. Given the choice, I think most people would rather enjoy this life as rich people who enjoy rich lives. And they can, if they are willing to pay the price.

CHAPTER TWO

WHAT IS THE PRICE OF A MISTAKE?

"My banker has never asked me for my report card."
— Rich dad

At the age of 15, I failed the subject of English because my spelling was horrible and I could not write. Or, I should say, my English teacher did not like what I wrote. That meant I would have to repeat my sophomore year.

The emotional pain and embarrassment came from many fronts. First, my dad was the superintendent of education for the island of Hawaii and in charge of over 40 schools. There was snickering and laughter throughout the halls of education as word spread from school to school that the boss's son was an academic failure. Second, failing meant I was going to join my younger sister's class. In other words, she was moving forward, and I was moving backward. And third, it meant I would not receive my athletic letter for playing varsity football, the sport for which I had played my heart out.

The day I received my report card and saw the F in English, I went behind the building that housed the chemistry lab to be alone. I sat down on the cold concrete slab, pulled my knees up to my chest, pushed my back up against the wooden building, and began to cry. I had been expecting this F for a few months, but seeing it on paper brought out all the emotions, suddenly and uncontrollably. I sat alone behind the lab building for over an hour.

The good news was that my best friend Mike, rich dad's son, also received an F. It wasn't good that he failed too, but at least I had company to go along with my misery. I waved to him as he headed across campus to catch his ride home, but all he did was shake his head and keep on walking.

That evening, after my siblings had gone to bed, I told my mom and dad that I had failed English and would have to repeat my sophomore year of high school. At that time, the educational system had a policy that required a student who failed either English or social studies to repeat the entire year. While they had expected this news, the confirmation of my failure was still a difficult reality.

My dad sat quietly and nodded. His face was expressionless. My mom, on the other hand, was having much more difficulty. I could see the emotions on her face—emotions that went from sadness to anger. Turning to my dad, she asked, "What's going to happen now? Will he be held back?"

All my dad would say in reply was, "That's the policy. I'll look into the matter."

For the next few days, my dad, the man I refer to as my poor dad, did look into the matter. My dad discovered that, out of my class of 32 students, the teacher had failed 15 of us. The teacher had given Ds to another eight students. One student received an A, four got Bs, and the rest Cs. Most of those who failed were the top students in the sophomore class. Most of us were on track to go on to college.

With such a high failure rate, my dad stepped in. He did not step in as my father, but as the superintendent of education. His first step was to order the principal of the school to open a formal investigation. There were mistakes made by both the students and the teacher. The investigation began with interviews of the students in the class. The investigation ended with the teacher being transferred to another school. A special summer school was offered to students who wanted an opportunity to improve their grades. I spent three weeks that summer working my way up to a D in English and was able to move on to the eleventh grade with the rest of my class.

My dad said to me, "Take this academic failure as a very important lesson in your life. You can learn a lot, or you can learn nothing from this incident. You can be angry, blame the teacher, and hold a grudge. Or you can look at your own behavior and learn more about yourself and grow from the experience. I don't think the teacher should have awarded so many failing marks. But I do think you and your friends need to become better students. I hope both the students and your teacher grow from this experience."

I must admit I did hold a grudge. To this day, I still don't like that teacher, and I hated going to school after that. I never liked being told to study subjects I was not interested in or knew I would never use once school was over.

Although the emotional scars were deep, I did buckle down a little more, my attitude changed, my study habits improved, and I graduated from high school on schedule. I was also one of two students from the state of Hawaii who were awarded a congressional appointment to the U.S. Merchant Marine Academy. I graduated from the academy in 1969 with a Bachelor of Science degree.

At the academy, I overcame my fear of writing and actually learned to enjoy it, although technically I am still a poor writer. I thank Dr. A. A. Norton, my English teacher for two years at the academy, for helping me overcome my lack of self-confidence, my past fears, and my grudges. If not for Dr. Norton, I doubt if I would have become a *New York Times* and *Wall Street Journal* best-selling author.

Most importantly, I took my poor dad's advice and made the best of a bad situation. Looking back, I can see how failing my English class and almost failing tenth grade was a blessing in disguise. The incident caused me to buckle down and make corrections in my attitude and study habits. I realize now that, if I had not made those corrections in the tenth grade, I would surely not have made it through the academy.

Rich Dad's Comments

The F in English that rich dad's son, Mike, received from the same teacher disturbed rich dad. He was grateful that my dad intervened and set up a summer-school program for us to make up our failing grades. Yet he used the experience to pass along a different lesson to Mike and me.

"Our lives are ruined," I said.

"What's the use?" added Mike. "We will never get ahead because of that teacher. On top of that, we have to spend our summer in a classroom."

Mike and I complained a lot after we failed English. In some ways, we felt our future, or at least our summer, had been taken away from us. We could see the so-called smart kids moving on, and we felt we were left behind. Many of our fellow classmates walked by us and snickered. A few called us "losers." Occasionally we heard behind our backs, "If you don't have good grades, you won't get into a good college." Or, "If you think high school English is hard, just wait till you get to college." We tried to handle the rude comments that are common among kids by laughing it off. Yet deep down, it still hurt. The truth was that we did feel like failures, and we did feel that we were being left behind.

One day after summer school, Mike and I were sitting in rich dad's office discussing our classmates' comments and how we felt about them. Rich dad overheard us, sat down, looked the two of us straight in the eyes, and said, "I'm tired of you two boys whining and complaining. I'm tired of you thinking like victims and acting like losers."

He sat there glaring at us. "Enough is enough. You failed. So what? Just because you failed once doesn't make you a failure. Just look at how many times I've failed. So stop feeling sorry for yourselves, and stop letting your classmates get to you."

"But we now have bad grades," I protested. "Those bad grades will stay with us forever. How will we get into a good college or university?"

"Look," said rich dad. "If you two boys let one bad grade ruin your life, you have no future anyway. If you let one bad grade be your downfall, then real life will beat you anyway. Real life is much tougher than high school English. And if you blame your English teacher and think that your English teacher was tough, then you have a rude awakening waiting for you when you enter the real world. The world outside of school is filled with people much harder, much tougher, and much more demanding than your English teacher. If you let one bad grade and one English teacher ruin your future, then you have no future anyway."

"But what about the kids who are teasing us and laughing at us?" asked Mike.

"Oh, come on," said rich dad with a chuckle that soon broke into a laugh. "Look at how many people criticize me! Robert, look at how many times your dad has been publicly criticized. Look at how many times both our names have been in the news. How many times have I been called a greedy businessman? And how many times has your dad been called an unfair public servant? If you two let a bunch of kids with pimples on their faces get to you and defeat you, then you really will be failures."

Rich dad continued, "One difference between a successful person and an average person is how much criticism they can take. The average person cannot take much criticism, and that is why they remain average all their lives. That is why they fail to become leaders. Average people live in fear of what someone else may say or think of them. So they live their lives trying to get along with all the other average people—living in fear of criticism, in fear of what someone else might think of them. People are always critical of other people. Look, I criticize your dad, and I know he criticizes me. Yet we still respect each other.

"But if people are criticizing you, at least they've noticed you. Be worried if no one is criticizing you," rich dad concluded with a laugh. "You two have given them something to talk about. You've given them something to break the boring monotony of their lives. If you can learn to handle criticism, you are learning something valuable for your life," rich dad said, still laughing.

"Look, one third of the people will love you no matter what you do. One third of the people will dislike you regardless of what you do, good or bad. And one third of the people won't care either way. Your job in life is to ignore the one third who will never like you and do your best to convince the one third in the middle to join the one third who love you. That's it. The only thing worse than being criticized is not being criticized." He laughed heartily at himself.

"So even grown-ups live in fear of other people and being criticized?" I asked, doing my best to get back to the lesson and away from rich dad's laughter. He thought it was funny, but I didn't see the humor.

Rich dad nodded and grew more serious. "It's the number-one fear of most humans. It's called the fear of ostracism—the fear of being different, of standing outside the herd. That is why public speaking is the number-one fear, a fear greater than death for many people."

"So people just join the herd and hide in the herd because they are afraid of being criticized?" Mike asked.

"Yes, and that is one reason so few people ever achieve great wealth. Most people feel safer in the herd of the average, living in fear of being criticized or being different," said rich dad. "Most people find it easier to be average, to be normal, to hide, doing exactly what the herd does—just going along to get along."

"What you are saying is that this whole affair of failing English class could be a very good thing for us in the long run?" Mike asked.

"If you want to make it a good thing," replied rich dad quietly. "Or you can make it a bad thing."

"But what about our grades? Those grades will go with us for the rest of our lives," I added with a slight whine.

Rich dad shook his head and then leaned over and said sternly, "Look, Robert. I'll share with you a big secret." He paused to make sure I was hearing his communication directly and without distortion. He then said, *"My banker has never asked me for my report card."*

His comment startled me and jolted me out of my chain of thinking—the chain of thought that was saying my life was ruined because of bad grades.

"What are you saying?" I responded feebly, not fully understanding where he was going with this statement.

"You heard me," rich dad said, sitting back in his chair. He knew I heard him. He was letting his statement sink in. He knew that it was shaking a core value of my family, a family of educators. In my family, report cards and good grades were almost sacred.

"Your banker has never asked you for your report card?" I asked quietly. "Are you saying that grades aren't important?"

"Did I say that?" asked rich dad. "Did I say grades aren't important?"

"No," I replied sheepishly. "You didn't say that."

"So what did I say?"

"You said, 'My banker has never asked me for my report card.'"

"When I see my banker, he does not say, 'Show me your grades,' does he?" rich dad asked, without waiting for an answer.

"Does my banker ask, 'Were you a straight-A student?' Does he ask me to show him my report card? Does he say, 'Oh, you had good grades. Let me lend you a million dollars.'? Does he say things like that?"

"I don't think so," said Mike. "At least he has never asked you for your report card when I was with you in his office. And I know he does not lend you money based on your grade-point average."

"So what does he ask for?" asked rich dad.

"He asks you for your financial statement," Mike replied quietly. "He always asks for balance sheets and updated P&Ls, profit-and-loss statements."

Rich dad continued, "Bankers always ask for a financial statement. Bankers ask everyone for a financial statement. Why do you think they ask everyone, rich or poor, educated or uneducated, for a financial statement before they will lend them any money?"

Mike and I shook our heads silently and slowly, waiting for the answer. "I've never really thought about it," said Mike, finally. "Why don't you tell us?"

"Because your financial statement is your report card once you leave school," rich dad said in a strong, low voice. "The problem is that most people leave school and have no idea what a financial statement is."

"My financial statement is my report card once I leave school?" I asked incredulously.

Rich dad nodded his head. "It's one of your report cards—a very important report card. Other report cards are your annual health checkup, your weight, your blood pressure, and the emotional health of your marriage."

"So a person could have straight As on their report card in school and have Fs on their financial statement in life?" I asked. "Is that what you are saying?"

Rich dad agreed. "It happens all the time. Often, people who have good grades in school have poor to average financial grades in life."

Good Grades Count in School; Financial Statements Count in Life

Receiving a failing grade at age 15 turned out to be a valuable experience for me because I realized I had developed a bad attitude toward my studies. It was a wake-up call to make corrections. I also realized early in life that, while grades are important in school, my financial statements would be my report card once I left school.

Rich dad said to me, "In school, students are given report cards once a quarter. If a child is in trouble, the child at least has time to make the proper corrections if he or she wants to. In real life, many adults never receive a financial report card until it's too late. Because many adults do not have a quarterly financial report card, many adults fail to make the financial corrections necessary to lead a financially secure life. They may have a high-paying job, a big home, a nice car, and they may be doing well at work, yet they are failing financially at home. They may be too old or out of time when they finally realize they have failed financially. That is the price of not having a financial report card at least once a quarter."

Learn from Your Mistakes

Neither of my dads liked the fact that their sons failed in school. Yet neither dad treated us as failures. Instead, they encouraged us to learn from our mistakes. As my schoolteacher dad said, "'Fail' is a verb, not a noun."

Unfortunately, too many people think that when they fail, they become a noun and call themselves "failures." If people choose to learn from their mistakes, just as children learn to ride bicycles by falling off bicycles, whole new worlds will open up. If they go along with the herd of people who avoid making mistakes, or lie about them, or blame someone else for their mistakes, then they fail to take advantage of the primary way human beings were designed to learn—by making mistakes and learning from those mistakes.

If I had not failed my English class at age 15, I might never have graduated from college, and I doubt that I would have learned that the report card for life after school would be my personal financial statement. That mistake at age 15 was priceless in the long run. The reason so few people achieve great wealth is simply because they fail to make enough mistakes. Mistakes can be priceless if we are willing to learn from them.

People who have made a mistake but have not yet learned the lesson from that mistake are often people who continue to say, "It wasn't my fault." Those are the words of a person who is wasting one of life's greatest gifts, the gift of making a mistake. Our jails are filled with people who continue to say, "I'm innocent. It wasn't my fault." Our streets are filled with people who lead unfulfilled lives because they continue to repeat what they were taught at home and in our schools: "Play it safe. Don't make mistakes. Mistakes are bad. People who make too many mistakes are failures."

When I speak to a group of people, I often say, "I am in front of you today because I have made more mistakes than most of you and I have lost more money than most of you." In other words, the price of becoming rich is the willingness to make mistakes, to admit you made a mistake without blaming or justifying, and to learn from those mistakes. The people who often have the least success in life are those who are unwilling to make mistakes or who have made mistakes and have not yet learned the lessons. So they get up each morning and continue to make the same mistakes, never learning from them.

CHAPTER THREE

WHAT IS THE PRICE OF EDUCATION?

"You can only invest two things: time and money."
– Rich dad

I am occasionally asked, "Are you saying that a person does not need to go to school?"

I answer emphatically, "No, I am *not* saying that. Education is more important today than ever before. What I am saying is that the educational system is behind the times. It is an old Industrial-Age system that is trying to cope with the Information Age. Unfortunately, it is not doing a very good job of coping."

According to economic historians, in 1989 when the Berlin Wall came down and the World Wide Web went up, the Industrial Age ended and the Information Age officially began.

Here is a simple example of this change:

Industrial Age	**Information Age**
Job security	Financial security
Job for life	Free agents
One profession	Many professions

Defined-benefit pension plans
    Employer is responsible.
	Defined-contribution pension plans—401(k)
	    Employee is responsible.

Social Security is certain.	Social Security is uncertain.
Medicare is certain.	Medicare is uncertain.
Seniority is an asset.	Seniority is a liability.

Pay raises are based upon tenure.	Pay raises are a liability.
	    Employers are looking for younger
	    workers with more current technical skills
	    willing to work for less money.

Why Job Security Is Not a Problem

My mom and dad grew up during the Great Depression. That historical event affected their mental and emotional outlook. That is why they often emphasized the importance of "getting good grades so you can get a safe, secure job."

Today, the issue is financial security, not job security. In large part, this is due to the shift from the employer paying for retirement through defined-*benefit* Industrial-Age pension plans to now the employee paying for retirement through defined-*contribution* Information-Age pension plans.

There are three major problems with today's defined-contribution pension plans.

1. *They are to be funded by the employee.*
   Many employees are not putting any money into their plans because they need the money to live on.

2. *The plans are indexed to the stock market.*
   If the stock market is high, the pension plan is high.
   If the market crashes, so will the employee's pension plan.

3. *A defined-contribution pension plan can run out of funds just when the retiree needs the money the most.*

Let's say the retiree is 85 years old and their retirement fund is depleted. The former employer has no obligation to the retiree. In contrast, the old defined-benefit retirement plan of the Industrial Age would have supported the employee until the employee died, regardless of age.

My biggest concern is the government's Social Security and Medicare programs. Of the two, the threat to the Medicare system in America concerns me most. As we get older, our living costs may go down, but our medical expenses skyrocket. One catastrophic illness could cost more than the person's home.

Today, a growing reason behind many personal bankruptcies is not financial mismanagement, but catastrophic illnesses. A friend of a friend of mine was injured in an auto accident. He was the sole breadwinner in the home, had inadequate medical insurance, and had to sell everything he owned to pay his medical expenses. To make matters worse, his youngest daughter was diagnosed with leukemia, and the family is now seeking charitable donations and assistance from anyone who will help.

What Is Lag Time?

Lag time means the time between a new idea's conception and its acceptance by the industry. In the world of business, the two industries with the longest lag times are the education industry and the construction industry. In the computer industry, the lag time is about a year. In the aerospace industry, the lag time is two years. That means it takes only two years for a new idea to be conceived and then adopted by the industry. In the education and construction industries, the lag time is approximately 50 years.

Many people are hoping the educational system will catch up to the idea that the Industrial Age is over. I doubt they will realize this until the year 2040, which is one reason why so many parents are pulling their kids out of school and choosing to homeschool.

Not only can industries be in lag, but individuals can also be in lag. In the Industrial Age, Einstein's $E = mc^2$ was the formula of the era. During the Industrial Age, there were two superpowers in charge, and people lived in fear of nuclear war between them.

In the Information Age, the World Wide Web has left no one in charge. Moore's Law is now in charge. Moore's Law states that information and technology are advancing quickly, doubling every 18 months. That means that each of us needs to double our information every 18 months, or risk falling behind. That is why, in the Information Age, *what* you learn is not as important as *how fast* you learn. Today it is risky to receive advice from anyone with old information. In the Information Age, "old" can be as short as 18 months. You don't want to be taking advice from someone who is lagging, or has old answers. Old answers may work on the millionaire trivia game shows, but they will not work in the real world.

So What Kind of Education Do We Need in the Information Age?

In many ways, both of my dads were great educators. They taught what they thought was important, but they did not teach the same things. Below is a list I created that summarizes the education I received from both dads. Although there are many different types of education—for example, physical education, music and art education, and spiritual education, all of which are important—the following are the three fundamental types of education that are required for minimal security in the Information Age.

1. *Academic*
    The education that teaches you how to read, write, and do arithmetic.

2. *Professional*
    The education that teaches you the skills to work for money, such as learning to be a doctor, lawyer, plumber, secretary, electrician, or teacher.

3. *Financial*
The education that teaches you how to have money work hard for you.

Obviously, all three types of education are vital. If one is not able to read, write, or do mathematics, life in general is very hard. Unfortunately, many students are leaving school today not well skilled in these fundamentals.

On May 7, 2000, the *Arizona Republic* ran an article that began with the headline, "LA Schools to Hold Back Thousands." Paraphrasing, the article made the following points:

- The nation's second largest school system backed down from plans to fail huge numbers of students this year.

- Los Angeles Unified School District officials originally expected to hold back as many as one third of the system's 711,000 students, but the promotion guidelines were relaxed, out of concern that mass failures could cripple schools.

That is correct. They needed to fail nearly a quarter of a million students because they could not attain basic reading, writing, and arithmetic standards. Officials passed the students because the failures would cripple the schools. I wonder what this will mean to a student who is academically crippled for life?

This is an example of an industry in lag. Obviously, students have changed, but the school system continues with its traditional ways of attempting to educate. Personally, I found school boring and irrelevant. I was not motivated by the idea that I needed good grades for job security, as my parents had been motivated. Academic education is more important than ever before, but our educational system fails to keep pace with the times, so a student's education is sacrificed while we wait for the system to change and catch up.

At one time, my real dad was the head of the teachers union in Hawaii. Because of him, I understand why the union is important to the teachers, and I do empathize with many of the teachers' concerns.

I also empathize with the students and am concerned about the long-term impact of their not receiving an adequate education when education is now more vital than ever.

When you look at professional education, its importance is also striking. For example, a person with only a high school diploma may earn $10 per hour right out of school. If that same person should go to electrician's school, their hourly rate could easily jump to $50 or more. When you multiply that difference of $40 per hour by eight hours a day, five days a week, 52 weeks a year, over 40 years, the investment in professional education may be one of the best returns on time and money anyone can make. When you understand that most medical doctors invest an extra 10 to 15 years beyond high school to become a doctor, it is no wonder that they feel they deserve a little bit more in pay than the rest of us.

Whether you do well in school or not, or whether you go on to become a doctor or a janitor, we all need basic financial education. Why? Because regardless of what we do or who we become, we all handle money. I have often wondered why we do not teach much about money in school. I have often wondered why the system focuses so much on grades and report cards when, in the real world, my banker has never asked me to submit my report card.

I often ask educators these questions. They give responses such as, "We do teach economics in school," or "Many of our students learn to invest in the stock market," or "We offer a junior business program for students who are interested in business."

I realize that the people in the system are teaching what they know and doing the best they can. Yet if you ask most bankers, they will tell you that they are looking for more than a stock portfolio or the student's grades in economics.

For most people, highly educated or not, it is not what they know that is costing them money. It is what they do *not* know that is costing them money.

Let's take just one subject to illustrate the lack of financial education: taxes. Most of us realize that taxes are our single largest expense. We are taxed when we earn, spend, save, invest, and die. Now, compare the large percentage of taxes an employee pays to the smaller percentage a business owner pays. The difference in dollars over 40 years is staggering. One of the reasons why so many people who "go to school, get good grades, and get a good job" struggle financially is simply because most of their money goes to the government—the same government that educates us, or fails to educate us. And taxes are just one small subject in the vast world of financial education.

Now compute the cost of what happens to a person who cannot read a financial statement and doesn't even know what a financial statement is. Or what happens to a person who does not know the difference between an asset or a liability; good debt and bad debt; debt versus equity; or the difference between passive income, earned income, or portfolio income. It is the lack of this basic financial knowledge that undermines a person's basic financial intelligence. It is this lack of financial intelligence that causes many people to work hard professionally, earn a lot of money, but fail to get ahead financially. They may have job security, but may never find financial security.

My rich dad often said, "Financial intelligence is not how much money you make, but how much money you keep, how hard that money works for you, and how many generations you pass that money on to."

One of the main reasons that poor and middle-class kids start with a financial handicap in life is that their parents pass nothing on to them financially. It's almost impossible to include your job and your company pension plan in your will. I know, because my parents left very little money for us kids to move forward on, while rich dad gave his children millions of dollars in financial head starts. It is estimated that when John Kennedy Jr. died, he passed on hundreds of millions of dollars to each of his sister Caroline's two children.

Take a moment to think how different your life might have been if you had been given a $100-million head start? What could you have done with your life rather than get up and go to work?

Basic Financial Education

When people ask me, "What do I need to know financially?" I always reply, "Find out from your banker what is important to him or her, and you will know what is important financially." And that is why one of the best mistakes I ever made was to have bad grades in high school. If I had not received those bad grades in high school, I might never have realized that my banker does not think my grades are important. My banker only asks me for my financial statement and, as I said, most students leave school not knowing what a financial statement is. Most people simply fill out the financial statement the bank provides them, instead of submitting their own prepared financial statements.

Most people think that borrowing money means begging for money, rather than showing the banker why he or she should lend you money. Always remember that a banker's job is to lend you money, not turn you down. Bankers don't make money unless they lend you money. That is why, when a banker turns you down, it is like a teacher saying to you, "You have failing grades." Instead of getting angry at the banker, it is really a good time to ask him or her what you are *not* doing correctly and what you can do to improve your financial statement—your real report card once you grow up and leave school.

What Is Important on Your Financial Statement?

Different people look for different things on a financial statement. A financial statement is like reading the story of a person's life. It shows the reader how financially smart or financially ignorant a person is with their money. The following are some of the things my rich dad taught me to look for on financial statements. The financial statement used is from my *CASHFLOW 101* board game, which I created to teach financial literacy and the basics of investing.

The Three Types of Income

My rich dad taught me the importance of the three different types of income:

1. Ordinary earned
2. Portfolio
3. Passive

Today, when I look at an individual's financial statement, I can usually tell if the person is going to be rich, poor, or middle class, just by looking at the income column.

This is the financial statement from *CASHFLOW 101*. It teaches people how financial statements work.

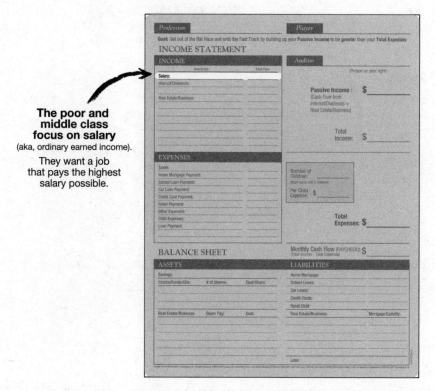

The poor and middle class focus on salary (aka, ordinary earned income).

They want a job that pays the highest salary possible.

The previous financial statement is of someone who manages their money like a poor or middle-class person because the only kind of income shown is ordinary earned income, their salary, which is by far the hardest income to get rich on. It's close to impossible to get rich on ordinary earned income because every time this person gets a pay raise, so does the government. Furthermore, if the person stops working, the ordinary earned income also stops.

The following financial statement shows a person who has a good chance of becoming richer and richer. Why? Because this person has passive income from assets such as businesses and real estate, the least-taxed income there is. They also have portfolio income from paper assets such as stocks and bonds and other investments.

A financial statement of a person getting richer by focusing on assets creating passive income:

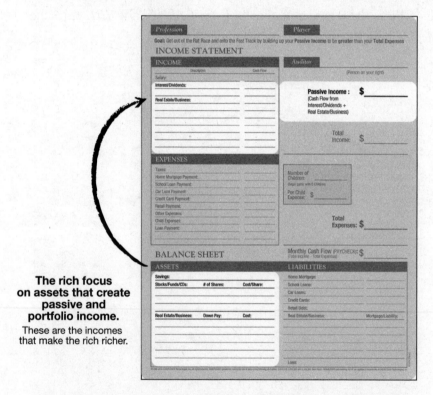

The rich focus on assets that create passive and portfolio income.

These are the incomes that make the rich richer.

The Kennedy kids never needed jobs. They never needed a paycheck. Why? Because the older Kennedy generation knew that portfolio income and passive income are the incomes of the rich. The Kennedy children chose to work, but they did not need to. If you had a $100-million portfolio, the passive and portfolio income would be more than enough to live a lifestyle of the rich and famous.

The *CASHFLOW 101* game is important for anyone serious about becoming rich because the game teaches people how to convert ordinary earned income, the income of the poor and middle class, into passive and portfolio income, the incomes of the rich. It is virtually impossible to become rich only on ordinary earned income. Unfortunately, that is what most people are trying to do.

More importantly, the game teaches how a financial statement works, which is something that cannot be learned by reading a book or by just playing the game a few times. Since repetition is the way we learn, playing the game repeatedly can assist players in mastering the technicalities of a financial statement, which is your report card once you leave school. By repeatedly learning how a financial statement really works, the game also reinforces the importance of passive and portfolio income, the income of the rich. It also teaches the difference between good debt and bad debt. By repeatedly playing the game, you begin to break up the core programming of working hard for money, which most of us learned at home and at school. The game trains your brain in the concepts of how money can work for you.

Complaints about CASHFLOW 101

Let me share with you the three most common complaints about the *CASHFLOW 101* game:

1. *It takes a long time to learn.*

   I recommend dedicating two four-hour sessions to learn the basics of the entire game: three hours playing and one hour reviewing the lessons learned with the rest of the players. Players report that the one-hour review sessions, or "debriefs," are the best part of playing the game. In those review sessions, the players relate the game to their real-life financial challenges. After the two sessions, you are better able to try different financial strategies in order to win the game. The game is much like the game of chess, which means there is not a single formula for winning. Each time the game is played, it will offer you different financial challenges. By solving the different financial challenges each game presents, your financial intelligence increases.

2. *It takes too long to play.*

   The game does take a long time, especially when a person first begins to learn. But the length of playing time decreases when the player learns how to solve the different challenges each game presents. The object of the game is to consistently see if you can complete the game in about an hour. In other words, the length of playing time decreases as your financial intelligence increases.

3. *It costs too much.*

   The *CASHFLOW* game is an educational tool created only for people who are serious about their financial education. In a market study, when the game was less expensive, people perceived it only as an entertainment game rather than as a total educational package.

The *CASHFLOW* games are only for those who are serious about their financial education. As rich dad said, "You can only invest two things: time and money." Most people are not willing to invest either time or money in their financial education, and that is why only 1 out of 100 people will achieve great wealth by age 65.

Who Grades Your Test?

One of the important reasons for receiving a report card in school is to give you an indicator on how well you are doing and what you need to correct. By not knowing that your financial statement is your report card once you leave school, many people never really know how well they are doing financially. Many people fail to maximize their income potential and wind up struggling financially most of their lives.

My poor dad, a straight-A student in school, did not really find out he had failed financially until he lost his job at age 50. The sad part was, although he knew he was in financial trouble at age 50, he did not know what to do about it. All he knew was that money was going out faster than it was coming in. That is the price of not knowing how to prepare and read a financial statement and how to self-correct after you experience a financial failure. By playing *CASHFLOW*, you will better understand the importance of your financial statement, your report card for life.

Again, turning to the financial statement from *CASHFLOW 101*, you'll notice the line that reads *Auditor.*

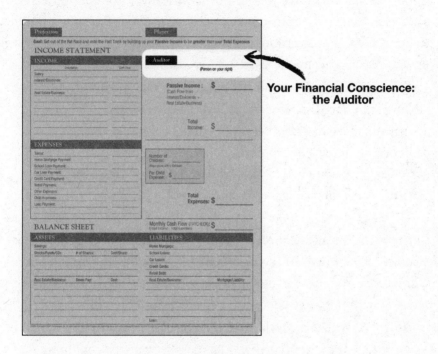

Your Financial Conscience:
the Auditor

Many times, when I have supervised the game being played in a seminar, I notice that players fail to fill out the line for the auditor. When I ask them why they left it blank, they often respond with, "Is it important?" Or, "I don't need to have anyone check my work." At that point, I become more stern, letting them know that the auditor, in this case another player in the game, is one of the most important aspects of the game. The game is designed to reinforce good financial habits, and having your financial statements checked on a regular basis is a financial habit essential for anyone who wants to become rich. In many ways, your auditor is like your teacher in school who goes over your work on a regular basis, letting you know how you are progressing, and helping you make any necessary corrections.

My wife Kim and I go through this financial-auditing process twice a month as a habit. Our accountant comes in, our financial statements and checkbooks come out, and the details of our financial life are reviewed in detail—twice every month. When we were struggling and short of cash, this process was a painful one. It was like looking at a report card filled with Ds and Fs. But as we learned from our mistakes, corrected them, and improved our financial situation, the twice-monthly auditing sessions became fun. It must be like receiving a report card with straight As, an academic pleasure I never knew.

When Kim and I first started out together in 1985, we were looking at financial statements with very little on them. Debt from my past financial disasters was heavy in the liability column and we had nothing in the asset column. It was very unpleasant to look at our financial statements. It was like looking at an x-ray of a cancer patient—only, for me, it was financial cancer.

Today my entries in the asset column are substantial. The number of entries in the income column of ordinary earned, passive, and portfolio income has increased, and so has the number of zeros after each number. Our income from passive and portfolio income is much greater than the expenses in our expense column.

In 1985 we had to work to survive, but today we work because we want to work. I doubt this would have been possible without the financial education my rich dad gave me. Without his teaching, I would not have known about the importance of a financial statement. I would not have known the difference between ordinary earned, portfolio, and passive income. I would not have known the importance of corporations and how to protect my assets and minimize taxes. I would not have realized the importance of a twice-monthly audit and why being tested and graded twice a month is essential to becoming financially free. That twice-monthly audit is just part of the price. With the financial education my rich dad provided to me, I became rich without cutting up my credit cards, winning the lottery, or going on a game show.

My Income Column Today

Today, Kim and I have an income column that looks like this:

Ordinary earned income	10%
Portfolio income	20%
Passive income	70%

A few days ago, a newspaper reporter asked me, "How much money do you make? How much is your paycheck?"

I replied, "Not much. I would rather not tell you how much my paycheck is. I'll just say that it is probably not as much as your paycheck."

He shook his head and smirked. "Then how can you write a book on money?" He went on to say that he hated writers who wrote about relationships but had no relationships, and writers who wrote about money who had no money. The interview was over, and he left.

Now that you are more financially educated, you may understand why I replied the way I did. My paycheck is very small because my paycheck is ordinary earned income, the highest-taxed income. Why would I want a larger paycheck when the government will only take a larger share of it? I would rather have more passive and portfolio income that I can keep for myself.

One of the biggest advantages of becoming financially educated is the tremendous amount of control you gain over the amount you pay in taxes, your single largest expense.

Professional Income

Another point to notice is that my income today does not come from my professional education. After graduating from high school, I attended the U.S. Merchant Marine Academy where I trained to be a ship's officer on tankers, freighters, and passenger ships. I also attended a U.S. Navy flight school at Pensacola, Florida, where I trained to be a professional pilot. Today, none of my income is derived from those two professions.

A lot of my passive income comes from a subject I failed in school. At the age of 15, if you recall, I almost failed my sophomore year because I could not write well. Because of that failure, I improved and today I am better known as an author than as a pilot or a ship's officer. The difference is measured in the millions of dollars. In other words, I have made much more money from my failures than from my successes.

In the Information Age, many of us will have more than one profession. That is why the issue is not *what* you learn, but *how fast* you learn. Remember Moore's Law which infers that information doubles every 18 months.

The number of answers you got right or how good your grades were in school does not measure your success later in life. Your success is measured by how many answers you do *not* know, how many times you fail, stand up, learn from your mistakes, make corrections without blaming, lying, or justifying, and then move on.

Definition of a Loser

If you want to find out what is important for your financial report card, simply go see your local banker. Fill out your personal financial statement and hope he or she rejects you. If they don't reject you, simply ask for more money. After they reject you, sit down and ask them what you can do to improve your financial report card. The education you receive could be priceless and life-changing. As I said, if you want to find out what is important in the real world, ask your banker. They look at people's report cards every day.

But the question is this: If bankers know so much, why aren't they rich? Why are they still working for the bank, minding someone else's business?

The answer is found in Newton's law which I covered earlier in this book. Newton's law states: For every action, there is an equal and opposite reaction.

The answer is also found in the explanation that to be a good, honest, and successful policeman, a policeman must also know how to be a good crook. Or that every coin has two sides, a bird has two wings, and we have two legs, arms, eyes, and so forth.

The reason most bankers are not rich is because they are too conservative. In order to be rich, especially if you start with nothing, you will need to be a good gambler as well as a good banker, and most good bankers are not good gamblers. As rich dad said, "You have to pay twice the price." To be rich, you have to pay the price of being both a good banker and a good gambler. Most people are neither.

Rich dad said to Mike and me, "The reason most bankers are not rich is because most bankers are not gamblers. And the reason most gamblers are not rich is because most gamblers are not good bankers."

I then asked him, "Are most people one or the other? Either a gambler or a banker?"

He replied, "No. Unfortunately, most people are financial losers."

"Losers?" I recoiled. "Isn't that a very harsh thing to say about people?"

"I said financial losers," rich dad replied in his defense. "I don't mean to insult anyone. Let me give you the definition of a loser before you think of me as unkind."

"Yes, please give me your definition," I replied, also a little defensively.

"My definition of a loser is someone who cannot afford to lose," said rich dad.

"Someone who cannot afford to lose?" I repeated, doing my best to understand rich dad's definition.

"Let me explain further," said rich dad calmly. "When it comes to money, most adults cannot afford to lose. Many people today live on what I call 'the red line.' As you know from your interest in cars, the car's red line is that point where the engine's rpm's are so high that, if you step on the gas any harder, the engine comes apart."

"So every dollar that is coming in as income is going out as an expense," Mike jumped in.

"That's correct," said rich dad. "So they cannot afford to lose because financially they have already lost." Rich dad paused to read our eyes and then said, "It's very sad. Millions of people all over this country, the richest country in the world, live at their financial red line."

"And," I concluded, "those are often the people who say, 'Investing is risky,' or 'What if I lose my money?' People often say such things or cling to their money extra tightly because they know they have already lost the financial battle."

Rich dad nodded. "You see, a true gambler realizes that winning and losing go hand in hand. Professional gamblers do not delude themselves that they can only win. True gamblers know that they can also lose. Gamblers know that they often lose in order to win."

"So that is why, if you want to be rich, you have to be a gambler as well as a banker," I added, beginning to understand more. The idea that a good cop also needs to be a good crook began to make more sense.

"And that is why people who have good grades in school do not necessarily do well in the real world," said Mike. "Real life is not made up of right answers. Real life is made up of multiple guesses, some of which turn out to be right, and many of which wind up being wrong."

Rich dad nodded, adding, "And that is why so many of the richest people in the world were often people who made the most mistakes. J. Paul Getty was known for drilling many dry holes in his quest for oil. He was famous for dry holes. But what made him rich was that he finally drilled a hole that hit one of the biggest oil fields in the world. The same is true for Thomas Edison, the man who reportedly failed 10,000 times before inventing the electric light bulb. The reason I say most people are losers is simply because they live their lives unable to afford even one little failure. To be successful, you must be both a banker and a gambler so you can afford to lose, because every gambler knows that losing is part of winning."

I created my *CASHFLOW* game based on rich dad's teachings. In the game, you will learn how to be a banker as well as a gambler. Too many people today want to put their money in safe, risk-free investments. I am afraid that many of these people will wind up as the big financial losers in life. While they may never lose, they may also never really win. These are the people who plan on becoming rich by being frugal, safe, living below their means, and cutting up their credit cards. As rich dad said, "You can be rich by being cheap. The problem is that you're still cheap."

How Much Can You Afford to Lose?

One of the reasons so many people play the lottery is because most people can afford to lose a dollar. The reason so many people play the dollar slot machines in the casinos is because they can afford to lose a few dollars. The problem is that, for at least 60 percent of the American population, they cannot afford to lose much more than a few dollars. That's because they have already financially lost the game of life. Many people will not find out how badly they have lost until they lose their job or have to stop working due to age or medical disability. Hopefully, they will have family members who can afford to and are willing to take care of them.

These people live at their red line of life, deeply buried in bad debt. They are so concerned with survival that they cannot even imagine a life of wealth. The chapter called "Take Control of Your Cash Flow" in *Rich Dad's CASHFLOW Quadrant* book helps people start a plan for shedding their bad debt. If followed, the formula will help most people get out of bad debt within five to seven years. The six simple tips appear in this book in chapter 5, "How Much Debt Do You Really Have?"

These "red-line" people also believe that getting rich is a function of luck. At one of my talks, a person asked me this question, "How large a role does luck play in your finances?"

My reply was, "LUCK is an acronym for Laboring Under Correct Knowledge."

Recently, Kim and I lost $120,000 in a bad, very speculative investment. A close friend was very upset, almost as if it were *his* money. He said to us, "The two of you are unlucky." Kim and I did not say much in response because there is no real reason to speak to someone who lives in fear of losing. We did not tell him that we had also made about a million dollars and had lost only $120,000 in our portfolio.

We also did not tell him that we really felt lucky because of two reasons. Reason number one is that we learned a lot more from that $120,000 loss than from the million-dollar win. In other words, we gain more knowledge from our mistakes. The second reason is because we could afford to lose that much money and not feel bad about it. That would not have been true just a few years earlier.

CHAPTER FOUR

What Is the Price of Cutting Up Your Credit Cards?

"You must know the difference between good debt and bad debt."
— *Rich dad*

So what is wrong with cutting up your credit cards?

To me, cutting up your credit cards is like someone who needs to lose weight and goes on a crash diet. Faithfully, you diet for a month, living only on three carrot sticks per meal with four ounces of plain yogurt for dessert. After 30 days, you can't stand the pain any longer.

One day in the mall, a young worker from the cookie company offers you one small sample. The aroma of those fresh-baked cookies is overpowering to your senses, so you say to yourself, "Oh, go ahead. You've been good. Just have a small piece of that cookie." Suddenly, you find yourself buying a bag to "take home to the family," but the bag of cookies never leaves the shopping mall. The binge is on. Soon you are 10 pounds heavier than you were when you started the diet. The action of crash-dieting leads to the reaction of overindulging.

People who know me know that I do not have the answer for the yo-yo diet. If I had the diet that guaranteed permanent weight loss, I would be richer than Bill Gates. Unfortunately, I know only too well what it feels like to diet and then go back on an eating binge. In my family, I am the only one with a weight problem, a problem I have struggled with since childhood, so I cannot blame family genetics.

While I do not have the solution for instant weight loss, I do have a solution for binge spending and credit-card debt. And cutting up your credit cards is not the solution. My solution comes with a price. And once again, the question is, "Are you willing to pay the price?"

Beauty and the Beast

A friend of mine and his wife are models of physical beauty. They are slim, trim, and healthy. Dieting is not an issue for them. Working out at the gym is not a problem either.

Managing their money is a different story. Both are in their late forties and make a lot of money, but they also spend so much that it frightens most people who know them. They pay off their old credit-card bills with their new credit cards. When they max out their home-equity loans, they buy a bigger house. They have a full-time maid and a nanny for their kids. They have more cars, more toys, more clothes, more lavish vacations than people making 10 times more than they do. They work hard making a lot of money, but never deal with the real problem—their lack of financial restraint.

We have been great friends for years so when we get together, they lecture me about my lack of discipline with food and exercise, and I warn them about their lack of financial discipline. As I said earlier, we all have our different challenges in life. Mine is food, and theirs is money.

The Rich Have More Debt Than the Poor

I love spending money, but Kim and I are not foolish with our money. I love having the finer things in life. I love having the choice of flying first class or economy. I love tipping people well if they have given great service. I love giving bonuses when extra money comes into the company. I love making my friends rich when our investments do well. I love the freedom that money buys. I love working if I want to, and not working if I don't. So for me, money is fun, money buys me more choices and, most importantly, it buys Kim and me the *freedom* from the drudgery of earning a living. That is why I do not understand people who say, "Money does not make you happy." I often wonder what they do for fun.

When someone says, "Cut up your credit cards," I don't think it makes people happy. One of the main reasons people spend money is to make themselves happy. Now, there are people who carry the need for financial happiness to extremes, just as there are people who exercise and diet to extremes. But in my opinion, the main reason that cutting up credit cards does not work in the long run is because cutting back on things you enjoy does not make most people happy. Given the choice, people would rather have more money and the freedom to enjoy life more. The only people who say, "Money does not make you happy," are either people who already have a lot of money and are still unhappy, or people who would not know what being happy really is. In my opinion, people are unhappy when they're not able to pay their bills or don't have the money to do the things they would love to do.

In the late 1970s, my company made millions of dollars very quickly in my nylon-and-Velcro® surfer-wallet business. Being in my late twenties, the money and success went straight to my head or, should I say, to my ego. Each time I looked at the company's balance sheet and saw the money piling up, I felt more and more elated. I became cocky and arrogant. I thought that, with each dollar increase, my IQ increased also.

Unfortunately, it worked exactly the opposite for me. As my dollars were going up, my financial IQ was actually going down. Soon, I was into fast cars and faster women. The experience of fast cars and fast women was fun and I don't regret that time in my life, but it couldn't last. The pain of going from being a paper millionaire to suddenly being a person with nearly a million dollars of real debt was a sobering experience. That's why I am concerned with so many people today who feel rich because their portfolios are filled with paper assets. There is a very big difference between *paper* assets and *real* assets, *paper* wealth and *real* wealth.

After losing my first million, I went to rich dad to ask for his advice. Looking over my financial statement, all he could do was shake his head and finally say, "This is a financial train wreck." Then he proceeded to chew me out. As I said about the value of mistakes, that "financial train wreck" and the reprimand that followed were some of the best lessons of my life. The value from that mistake has been priceless and continues to serve me well today. Although that failure cost me nearly a million dollars, in the long run it also made me many more millions and will continue to make me even more money in the future.

Making a mistake and learning from it can be a priceless experience. However, making a mistake and then lying, blaming, denying, or pretending you did not make a mistake is a waste of a good mistake. Today, when I find myself in the middle of a new mistake, I say to myself, "Keep your head. Don't blow your cool. Pay attention, and learn from this experience. This seemingly bad experience will serve you well if you are willing to learn from it. Pay attention and learn as much as you can while you're in the middle of it."

Becoming a paper millionaire in my late twenties and then becoming a loser with a million dollars in real debt was a horrible experience. I wish I could say I paid attention and truly appreciated the experience while the house of cards was coming down, but I didn't. I blamed, I lied, I denied, and I tried to run from my responsibilities. The good thing was that I had my rich dad, who pinned me down and made me stop blaming and start learning one of the biggest lessons of my life.

Good Debt Into Bad Debt

After my big learning experience and once rich dad was through chewing me out, he said, "You have successfully converted a million dollars of *good* debt into a million dollars of *bad* debt. Not too many people make such big mistakes. You can learn from this experience, or you can run from it. You choose." As I said, mistakes can be priceless experiences but, in the middle of one, it is often difficult to realize the value of your stupidity.

Nonetheless, that "financial train wreck," as my rich dad called it, was filled with valuable lessons. One of the most important lessons I learned was to face my mistakes, learn from them, and try not to repeat them. Because I chose to "face the music," that became the most important lesson in a chain of many important lessons.

Another important lesson was the difference between good debt and bad debt. I did not really understand the concept, at least not as clearly as I did at that moment. My rich dad had often cautioned me about good debt and bad debt. He would say, "Every time you owe someone money, you become an employee of their money." He would explain to his son and me that *good debt is debt that someone else pays for you. Bad debt is debt that you pay for with your own sweat and blood.* That was why he loved rental real estate. He would add, "The bank gives you the loan, but your tenant pays for it." I had heard the concept and I understood it intellectually, but now I was learning the difference between good debt and bad debt with my body, my mind, and my spirit.

Today when I see people simply rolling their credit-card debt into a home-equity loan, I cringe. They may think it's a good idea and the government offers you a tax break for doing so, but now I know better. I know that they have only converted very expensive short-term bad debt into less expensive long-term bad debt. It may bring them temporary relief, but it does not solve the problem. They have turned their credit-card debt into a second mortgage.

The word *mortgage* comes from the Old-French word *mort*, which means *death*. *Mortir* means "an engagement until death." Like my friends who work hard only to get deeper in debt, they continue to ignore the real problem or learn the hard lesson. Unless something changes, they will be "engaged until death" with bad debt.

After I lost everything, I felt terrible, blamed others for my mistakes, and wanted to run from my problems. Rich dad forced me to face my mistakes. Going over the numbers was a painful, yet very useful, process. By facing my mistakes, it was obvious that I could not possibly work hard enough to pay off all the debt. Most people only lose a little at a time, pushing the debt problem slowly forward. If you lose $100,000 or are $100,000 in debt, it is possible to physically work hard and pay off that much debt. But when you lose a lot more money, the pain and reality of a lot of bad debt is sobering. When I lost $1 million, I knew hard physical work was not going to cut it, at least with my limited earning capacity. It was life-changing for me.

Once rich dad calmed down, he looked at me and said, "You can walk away from this experience and pretend it never happened. Or you can make it the best experience of your life."

On that day back in 1979, rich dad taught me a lesson that has proven priceless. On that day he said, "The rich have more debt than the poor. The difference is that they have good debt, and the poor and middle class are loaded up with bad debt." Rich dad went on to say, "You should treat all debt, good or bad, the same way you treat a loaded gun—with a lot of respect. People who do not respect the power of debt are often financially wounded by it—sometimes killed. People who respect and harness the power of debt may become rich beyond their wildest dreams. As you now know, debt has the power to make you very rich, and it also has the power to make you very poor."

Harnessing the Power of Debt

There are many reasons that I do not join the bandwagon that says, "Cut up your credit cards, get out of debt, and live below your means." I don't say those things because I don't think that advice solves the problem for anyone who wants to be rich. For people who want to have a lot of money and enjoy the lifestyle that money can bring, simply cutting up your credit cards and getting out of debt does not solve that problem, nor does it necessarily make people happy. On just basic financial principles, I do agree that cutting up your credit cards is good advice for most people. But simply getting out of debt does not work for anyone who wants to become rich and enjoy life. If a person wants to become rich, a person needs to know how to get into more of the right kind of debt, learn how to respect the power of debt, and learn how to harness the power of debt. If people are not willing to learn how to respect and harness the power of debt, then cutting up their credit cards and living below their means is great advice. Either decision has a price tag attached.

A Great Used Car

A friend of mine came to the house a few months ago to show me his new car. "I got an amazing deal," he said. "I paid only $3,500 for it, put in $500 for some parts, and it runs great. I could easily sell it for $6,000." He then said, "Come on. Sit in it. Take it for a spin." Not wanting to be rude, I did as he requested and took the car for a ride around the neighborhood. At the end of the test drive, I smiled and said, "It's a great car." But silently I said to myself, "It needs a paint job, the interior smells of old cigarettes, and I would not want to own such a depressing vehicle." Taking back the keys, he smiled and said, "I know it's not a thing of beauty, but I paid cash for this so I have no debt." As he drove off, thick smoke poured from the exhaust.

If You Want to Get Richer, Buy a New Car

My wife Kim drives a beautiful Mercedes convertible. I drive a Porsche convertible. Even when we were broke, we drove a Porsche and a Mercedes or other fine cars. We did not pay cash. We borrowed money to buy them. Why? Let me explain with the following story, a story I often tell in my seminars. It is a story about good debt and bad debt and enjoying the finer things of life.

In 1995, I received a phone call from my local Porsche dealer. He said, "The car of your dreams is here." I immediately drove down to his showroom to look at a 1989 Porsche Speedster. I already knew that there were only 8,000 of this model made over a three-year period. In 1989, Porsche devotees were buying them, putting them on blocks, and storing them. If you could find a collector who would sell one, the asking price was $100,000 to $120,000 in 1989. But in 1995, I was looking at the rarest of all the 1989 Porsche Speedsters. This was Speedster Number 1, the first ever built of this model, and it had the Porsche turbo body, which means little except to a dedicated Porsche fan. Since it was the first one built, it was the model that the factory toured all over the world at auto shows and was the car used for the photo on the brochure. The car also came with a special plaque from the Porsche factory. In 1989, after the tour was over, this car was also put up on blocks and stored in a warehouse. When a collector decided to sell it in 1995, the dealer called me. The dealer knew it was the car I had been looking for. The car may have been used, but it had only 2,400 miles on it.

My wife Kim watched me go into a hypnotic state as I walked up to the car of my dreams. I sat in the car, took hold of the steering wheel, and inhaled deeply, smelling the rich scent of leather, which was still with the car. The car was absolutely flawless, and the color was perfect, a shade Porsche calls "metallic linen." Kim looked at me and asked, "Do you want it?" I responded with a nod of my head and a smile.

"Then it's yours," Kim said. "All you have to do is find an asset to pay for it." Again, I nodded, climbed out of the car, sniffed the tires, and smiled. It was the car of my dreams, and it was mine. We put a deposit on the car, arranged financing with the dealer, and I went out to find the asset that would pay for the car. In other words, I was going to find an *asset* to pay for my *liability* and use *good debt* to pay for the *bad debt*.

A little over a week later, I found a great piece of property, borrowed money to buy it, and the cash flow from the property paid for the debt on the Porsche. A few years later, the Porsche would be paid off, and I would still have the cash flow from the property. In other words, instead of getting poorer from having an expensive liability, I got richer *and* got the car of my dreams, which is still mine today. We did the same thing when my wife found the Mercedes of her dreams.

The Best Things in Life Are Free

There is a saying that goes, "The best things in life are free." And I agree. A simple smile can make so many people happy, and a smile costs nothing to give. A pat on the back with the single word,

"Congratulations," costs nothing and it can brighten up a person's whole day. A sunrise or full moon costs nothing to appreciate. So in my opinion, the best things in life are free. What I am talking about in this section are the finer things in life that cost money. The kind of happiness I am talking about is the happiness one finds from material things. I am not writing about inner happiness because material possessions cannot give you that if you do not already have it. Inner happiness is free—and priceless if you have it. While each of us has free access to our own inner happiness, not all of us find it.

The Importance of Standard of Living

If I were in high school, my friend's $3,500 bargain mobile would have been my dream car. I would have driven that car with pride and showed it off to all my friends. But when I was in my forties, driving around in a cheap car was not my idea of a dream. At issue is something called your "standard of living," which is a measure of your material happiness and satisfaction.

There are three reasons why being aware of your material happiness or changes in your standard of living is important.

1. *Your standards change.*
    As we age, our standards change because we are changing. If a person finds their tastes improving but their ability to afford their refinements in taste do not change, that person may begin borrowing and increasing their share of bad debt in order to afford these changes. If your standards change, especially to the more expensive side, it is important to find ways of increasing your income in order to afford those changes.

2. *It is important to respect these inner changes in material standards.*
    A person's inner happiness can be affected if their material standards change, but the person is not able to keep up financially with these changes. For example, I might be a happy high school boy with a $3,500 used car, but I would be an unhappy adult driving the same car I dreamed of in

high school. Today, I meet many people who lack inner peace because they have not kept up with the changes in their desire for the finer things in life. I meet many people who are unhappy, living below their means, trying to be happy by only buying things that are cheap and affordable, but below their personal standards.

3. *It actually costs less if you buy what you desire.*
    I am very happy with my car, and my wife is happy with hers. We may seem that we've spent more in satisfying our material standards, which includes our house and clothing, but, in the long run, we actually spend less in time and money because we buy what we want.

Lessons Learned

Years ago, my rich dad said, "Some people believe that God wants us to live frugally and avoid the temptations of the finer things in life. There are other people who believe that God created these wonderful things for us to enjoy. It is up to you to choose which view of God you want to believe in."

I share the story of my Porsche because I want you to have the wonderful material things this world has to offer—without sacrificing your financial well-being and winding up in financial hell. And I tell the story for the lessons that follow about abundance.

Lesson #1: The Importance of Good Debt and Bad Debt
As stated earlier, rich dad stressed the importance of financial literacy and the fact that your financial statement is your report card once you leave school. The following financial statement shows my assets buying my liabilities in the Porsche transaction.

My Assets Buy My Liabilities

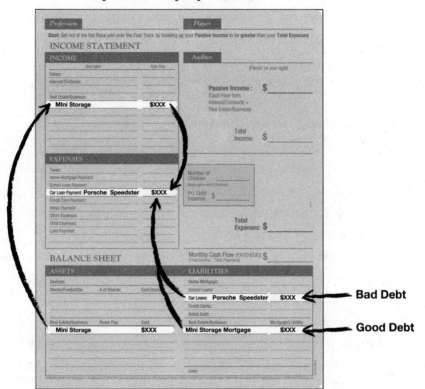

As you can see, I borrowed money for both the Porsche and the real estate investment—in this case, a mini-storage project in Texas. The cash flow from the investment covered the monthly costs of the Porsche. Because of good management, the cash flow from the mini-storage greatly increased and the Porsche was paid off two years early. Today, Kim and I have the real estate, the cash flow, and the Porsche. We used a similar process when buying her Mercedes. So we got richer while we were also able to drive the cars of our dreams. Our friends, the couple who live above their means and who drive the cars of their dreams, get poorer instead of richer because the income from their jobs is their only source of income. They look good physically on the outside, but I suspect that financial worries from bad debt are eating them alive on the inside. They are buying liabilities with bad debt instead of buying assets with good debt.

Buying assets with good debt that provide the cash flow for paying for the liabilities you want in life is what rich dad taught me. The cash flow from your assets represents your money working for you, something my friends and many people today still do not understand.

Whom Are You Really Working For?

When it comes to good debt versus bad debt, let me repeat what rich dad often said to me: "Every time you owe someone money, you become an employee of their money." That is, if you take out a 30-year loan, you've instantly become a 30-year employee. Unfortunately, they do not give you a gold watch when the debt is retired.

Rich dad did borrow money, but he did his best to not become the person who actually paid for the loans. That's the key. His advice bears repeating. He would explain to his son Mike and me that good debt was debt that someone else paid off for you, and bad debt was debt that you paid for with your own sweat and blood. His love of rental properties was based on "the bank gives you the loan, but your tenant pays it off for you."

Let me use a typical real-life example to illustrate just how this works. Assume that you find a nice little house for sale in a decent neighborhood. True, the home needs some fixing up— perhaps a new roof, new gutters, and maybe a new paint job. But by and large, it's surrounded by other homes that are fairly well maintained, the neighboring area is solid, and the schools are good. Even better, the neighborhood is right next to a local state university which is always looking for more student housing as the campus enrollment continues to increase year after year.

The homeowner wants to retire and move to someplace warm and sunny. He's asking $110,000 for his house. You negotiate a bit with him, and you finally settle on a price of $100,000. You already have $10,000 saved up in your bank account, so you need to get a mortgage for at least $90,000. But in truth, since that $10,000 is pretty much all the cash you have on hand, you decide to apply for a $100,000 mortgage. Why? Because with that additional $10,000, you can pay off the bank's closing costs as well as pay a local handyman to paint the house and repair the roof and gutters.

In many cases, the bank will be happy to give you the mortgage. Why? Because the mortgage is secured by the collateral value of the house. If you went to a bank and asked for a loan of $100,000 and you didn't have any collateral or secured assets to back it up, the bank would tell you to take a hike. But with the house property backing you up, the bank will usually help you finance the loan. Remember, the bank is in the business of making loans—and will do so when they know that there's real collateral to help secure that loan.

Let's move on. Under current finance rates, the bank gives you a 30-year mortgage at a rate of 6 percent. First, of course, they want that $10,000 cash as a down payment, which you give them. So, in addition to the $100,000 mortgage, your total investment is now $110,000.

Once you figure in your property taxes, your monthly mortgage payment is going to be about $700. But as mentioned before, you don't want to be an employee of that bank loan for the next 30 years. As long as you have that debt service, you're working for the bank. The better approach is to have someone else pay off that debt for you.

Rich dad would suggest that, once you close the deal and own the home, you then start talking to the local university about the possibility of students renting your home. Let's say that you charge $1,000 a month for the rent. If the home has four bedrooms, it could easily accommodate four students, each of whom would pay $250 a month. That's a fairly modest amount, even for the most cost-conscious student.

Or, you can simply check with a local real estate agency to see if they can handle the rental of your property. For a small monthly maintenance fee, many real estate agencies will not only find a renter for your property, but will also take care of any minor maintenance issues, such as fixing a clogged toilet.

Here's more good news. If your rental property is earning you $1,000 a month, and your mortgage payment is only $700, then your monthly net cash flow is $300 a month. This net income is what is known as *passive income*. That is, you're not doing any heavy lifting or hard labor to earn it. Someone else, your tenant, is paying off your 30-year mortgage for you, and even better, you're earning an extra $300 a month.

Rich dad's real estate investing philosophy is primarily based on cash flow. Do you have positive cash flow at the end of each month?

But there is also the popular philosophy that real estate generally goes up in value. While you're earning that extra income each month, you're also paying down your mortgage each month. That means that, very slowly but steadily, you are building more equity into the home. Since real estate properties may gain in value over time, your original investment of $110,000 in that home may also be appreciating in value. In other words, if 10 years from now you decide you want to sell the home, the market value of the house might have gone up to $125,000. So on paper, you would make a nice tidy profit of $15,000 from the sale of the house as well as all the passive income you collected.

But a word of caution from rich dad: "Always keep your eye on your cash flow. Look at potential appreciation in real estate as a bonus, not as a reason to buy."

Take a Tip from Those Who Have Taken Control

Take a look at the stories of everyday people who were fed up living paycheck to paycheck in the book, *Rich Dad's Success Stories*. They just got tired and frustrated of trying to count the years until they could retire and then theoretically live off their 401(k)s— assuming that their 401(k)s still had enough money in them to allow them to retire. In that book, you'll find easy-to-follow firsthand accounts of people—some as young as teenagers, some nearing retirement—who followed rich dad's advice and have started to develop steady streams of passive income.

Many of those success stories are built upon real estate investing. All of the people in the book explain how they had to overcome their fear of taking that initial leap of faith to find that first investment property. But invariably, once they started to see the stream of passive income develop, they almost all went back and repeated the process again—in many cases, again and again. Some of those folks have gone on from simple one-family properties to larger properties, and all of them point to rich dad's advice as having led the way for them.

In some of the success stories, the individuals decided to invest in small businesses in order to earn their financial freedom. One of the chapters profiles a woman who started to invest in laundromats. As soon as she and her husband found that it was a fairly safe and easy investment to make, they then invested in two more. Now, she and her husband are doing quite well financially, and they'll be the first to tell you that it was simply a matter of doing some financial homework and making their money work for them, instead of them working for money.

The point is that most people can't seem to get ahead financially because of the monthly onslaught of bills to pay. It's only when they finally make up their minds to do something about their financial lifestyle that they find the self-determination to look at other ways of generating money. And as rich dad says, "If you want to get out of the Rat Race, then you had better start learning about the different types of income: earned, portfolio, and passive." Whether it's investing in real estate, business, or other kinds of investments, the sooner you discover that there are lots of easier and better ways to make money than just having a job, the better off you and your family are going to be.

Lesson # 2: The Power of Inspiration

Let's get back to the used-car story. When I drove my friend's used car, I felt depressed. Sitting in the car did not inspire me. I did not hear angels singing or see the heavens open up with blessings as they had when I sat in my Porsche. As my friend drove away with smoke pouring out of the exhaust pipe, I felt nauseated. In contrast, when I open my garage door and look at my Porsche,

I still hear the angels singing. I love that car and I love the inspiration it gave me to go out and invest in another property. In other words, that car inspired me to get richer. Sitting in my friend's car only inspired me to take a bath.

I believe our Creator assists us humans in building beautiful things. When I see a beautiful painting or a beautiful home or a beautiful car, I feel inspired. I feel the generosity, the beauty, and abundance of God, and it inspires me to go out and invest more vigorously—by *investing* harder, not by *working* harder. I notice that people who treat themselves poorly are often not the most inspiring people to be around. I have some close friends who are so cheap that, when I am in their house, I feel like I am in my friend's used car. I love my friends dearly, and I do not impose my financial views on them. But they work hard at living below their means, while Kim and I work hard to continually expand our means. That makes a big difference in the way we live our lives. As I said, we are all different, and we make different choices in our lives. I am simply sharing with you how my wife and I use the luxuries of life to inspire us to become richer.

Lesson #3: My Banker Loves to Lend Me Money for Both Assets and Liabilities

My assertion in *Rich Dad Poor Dad* that your house is not an asset created a lot of controversy. In fact, I get more angry mail about that than any other point in my books. I often say, "When your banker says your house is an asset, they are not lying to you. They are just not saying whose asset it really is. Your house is *their* asset." I also state, "I'm not saying, 'Don't buy a house.' All I am saying is, 'Do not call a liability an asset.'" Still, the hate mail comes in.

Your banker will lend you money regardless of whether you buy an asset or a liability. Your banker does not tell you which one to buy. So if you want to buy a new speedboat and your financial statement shows that you can afford the payments, the banker will be more than happy to lend you the money. If you want to buy a three-bedroom home that you'll use as a rental property that makes you money and your financial statement is favorable, the banker again will generally lend you the money. Why? Because regardless of whether you borrow money for a liability or an asset, *to the banker, either one is an asset.* So people who first borrow money to buy assets usually end up with more money to buy liabilities. People who only buy liabilities often have no money left over to buy assets.

Since your banker does not really care whether you buy assets or liabilities, because either one is an asset to the bank, then maybe you should care. In fact, the more you care, the happier the banker is because the banker's job is to lend you more money, not turn you down for your loan. Bankers do not make money unless you borrow money. So the richer you become, the happier your banker also becomes. I love my banker because my banker lends me money to buy assets as well as liabilities.

Lesson #4: What Asset Does Your Banker Love the Most?
A radio host asked me, "What do you invest in?" I replied, "I began investing in real estate in my twenties, so the bulk of my investments is in real estate today. I also own businesses and some paper assets such as stocks and bonds."

The interviewer then said, "I don't like real estate. I don't want to fix toilets and receive phone calls late at night from tenants. That is why I don't invest in real estate. Everything I have is in stocks or mutual funds." He then ended the interview, cut to a commercial break, and I was ushered out of the studio.

An Expensive Idea
Later that evening, I reflected on that interview. I said to myself, "What an expensive decision that radio interviewer has made. He does not want to invest in real estate because he does not want to fix toilets or receive phone calls late at night. I wonder if he knows how much that single idea is costing him?"

The four primary asset classes a person can invest in are:

1. Businesses
2. Real estate
3. Paper assets
4. Commodities

As I sat there quietly that evening, I could hear rich dad saying to me, "Which one of the four asset classes does my banker love the most?" The answer is real estate. Of the four asset classes, it is very difficult to receive a loan to start a small business. You might get a small-business loan, but those loans often require you to pledge your other assets as security.

It is also very difficult to get your banker to lend you money to buy paper assets or commodities, especially for 30 years at a low interest rate. But your banker will loan you the money to buy real estate.

Years ago, rich dad said to Mike and me, "If you want to be rich, you must give your banker what he wants. First, your banker wants to see your financial statements. Second, a banker wants to lend you money to buy real estate. Just know what your banker wants, and you'll find it easier to become rich."

The radio host's prejudice against real estate was an expensive idea because he will have to use his own, after-tax dollars to buy his stocks, bonds, and mutual funds without being able to leverage his banker's money. He has to use the most expensive money of all, his own money that comes from his own labor, and only after the government has taken its share in taxes.

Let's use a $10,000 example to illustrate this point. If the radio host buys mutual funds, all he can buy is $10,000 worth. If the host were to buy real estate, he could buy a $100,000 property with the same $10,000 and $90,000 borrowed from the bank. If the property has a positive cash flow, the tenants' payments will cover all expenses and the cost of the bank's mortgage and will also provide some monthly income.

Let's say the markets are good and each asset goes up 10 percent that year. The mutual funds will gain $1,000 for that investor. The real estate will gain $10,000 for the investor, plus the monthly income from cash flow, plus depreciation. If the investor chooses to sell the property, there is no capital-gains tax in America if a tax-deferred exchange is used at the time of sale.

The mutual fund probably does not have any cash flow, is not entitled to depreciation benefits, and is taxed at a capital-gains tax rate if it is outside a retirement plan. (If it is inside a retirement plan, it will be taxed at the highest tax rate of all, the ordinary earned income-tax rate, when it is finally withdrawn.)

This is not to say that paper assets are bad, but to illustrate the cost of an idea such as, "I don't invest in real estate." To me, the biggest expense of all is personal freedom. For Kim and me, the best thing about real estate is the monthly passive cash-flow income, taxed at a lower rate than ordinary earned income, which allows us to be financially free. In other words, real estate allows us to have good debt, and good debt is debt that makes us richer quicker. But in utilizing leverage, the bank's money, to get richer quicker, there is a price to pay.

If you look at the returns on your capital using no leverage, your return on $10,000 is 10 percent. But by using the bank's money, your return is 100 percent on *your* money. The real estate market would need to go up by only 1 percent to have the same return as the paper market going up by 10 percent.

When you factor in the tax advantages, the real estate market can improve by less than 1 percent and have the same net return as a paper market improving by 10 percent.

Those are some of the reasons why rich dad said, "Always give the banker what he wants." And why he also issued these words of caution, "Always treat any debt as you would a loaded gun." That's because leverage can swing both ways with equal force. You can *make* a lot more money using the bank's money, and you can *lose* a lot more money using the bank's money. So the price to pay is an investment in your education and several years of experience. If you are not willing to pay that price, do not use other people's money.

Paying the Price for Education

In the 1970s, I invested in a real estate investment class which cost $385. That three-day course has been one of the best investments I have ever made. I started slowly with small investments and invested another five years in gaining the experience I needed. I do not want to fix toilets, nor do I want to receive phone calls late at night—and I don't. But I do like what my investment in real estate brings me, and that is a lot of good debt and a lot of freedom.

At a real estate seminar in Dallas, Texas, where I was the guest speaker, I was approached by a man about 60 years of age. He had heard me say, "My rich dad taught me to be a real estate investor by playing *Monopoly*®, and we all know the formula for great wealth found in that game: Buy four green houses, and turn them into one red hotel."

This gentleman came up to me and said, "Should I turn my houses into red hotels?"

I smiled and asked, "How many houses do you have?"

He thought for a moment and said, "A little over 700."

"What?" was all I could say in response.

Sitting down to find out more, I learned that he was a rancher in west Texas. For the last 40 years, he would buy a few houses a year and rent them out. He went through the booms and busts of both the oil and cattle businesses. When it was a bust economy, he would buy houses from people who were in financial trouble and often rent them back to them. As his cash flow grew, he just kept buying more houses, most under $65,000, and he never sold any. At the time of our meeting, I found out that he was averaging $200 a month per house in positive cash flow. I gasped and said, "You mean you have over $140,000 in monthly income? Over $1 million a year just from rental property?"

"Yup," he said. "That is why I came to ask you if you think I should start selling some of my green houses and start buying some red hotels. It takes a lot of time buying those little green houses. So I like your idea of buying bigger buildings. Then I don't have to buy as many."

I shook my head and laughed and said, "The next seminar we have, I want you to be the speaker, and I'll be the student." I then gave him the name and number of my financial and tax advisors and told him to call them. I told him that he was far beyond me.

As he thanked me for the phone numbers, my mind drifted back 40 years to memories of my rich dad playing *Monopoly*® with Mike and me. I was playing *Monopoly*® with little green plastic houses, and the gentleman walking away from me was playing the game for real. I could hear rich dad saying to Mike and me, "My banker always wants to lend me money to buy more real estate. So I always give my banker what he wants."

CHAPTER FIVE

What Is the Price of Getting Rid of Bad Debt?

"What do you do when you find yourself in a hole?
Stop digging."

– Anonymous

Before you can start on your way to financial freedom, you first have to pinpoint exactly how much bad debt you really have. For many people, figuring out how deeply in debt they are is like going to the dentist. You know it's good for you, but it's not always pleasant. Some people have already given up. They know they're in a big hole but don't want to deal with it.

But if you're serious about building positive cash flow in your life, you have to start with the fundamentals of financial literacy. Here's a quick quiz to get yourself going. Put a 1 next to any of the following questions to which you would answer yes:

_____ Do you routinely pay your bills late?

_____ Have you ever hidden a bill from your spouse?

_____ Have you neglected repairing the car because of insufficient funds?

_____ Have you bought something recently that you didn't need and couldn't afford?

____ Do you regularly spend more than your paycheck?

____ Have you been turned down for credit?

____ Do you buy lottery tickets in the hope of getting out from under your debt?

____ Have you put off saving money for a rainy day?

____ Does your total debt (mortgage excluded) exceed your rainy-day reserve?

Add up the numbers in the boxes. _____

- If your score is 0, that's great! You're already in control of your cash flow.

- If you scored in the 1–5 range, you may want to think about reducing your bad debt.

- If you scored in the 6–9 range, watch out! You may be headed toward financial disaster.

Rich Dad's Emergency Cash-Flow Program

If you really want to gain control of your cash flow, you're going to need three key ingredients:

1. A financial statement to know where you are financially
   (Use the financial statement from the *CASHFLOW 101* game, included in the Appendix, to fill out your own financial statement.)

2. Personal discipline

3. A game plan that's going to take you where you want to go

Is it difficult to change your habits? You bet it is. It depends on you, and how eager you are to take control of your financial life. Remember, you don't have to do any of these steps. But if you don't, you'll just remain where you are, in the current Rat Race of spending your paycheck on bills that never stop coming—unless, of course, you win the lottery. It's always amazing to me to see how many people think that winning the lottery is really a solid plan of getting ahead financially.

But let's get back to reality. While you don't have to cut up your credit cards, you do have to follow a debt-reduction plan. The first two steps in doing this are:

- **Pay yourself first.**
  Whenever you get a paycheck, the first bill you pay is to yourself. Not the car payment. Not the mortgage or rent money. Pay yourself a decent bit of money, and then immediately put that money into a separate investment savings account. And don't touch it until you're ready to invest it in some other way.

- **Cut back on what I call doodads.**
  Doodads are those extra things in life that we all crave but really don't need. It might be a fancy car or going out to dinner at expensive restaurants or really sharp clothes. Whatever your doodads are, just stop that habit of purchasing them impulsively. Admittedly, this is where your self-discipline and willpower come into play. But if you really want to get out of bad debt, you need to adopt the old-fashioned virtue of delayed gratification.

I am not changing rich dad's advice. While he believed in expanding your means to be able to afford any lifestyle you want, there are times when you have to stop and take other measures to get started on the right track. Remember that old saying: "What do you do when you find yourself in a hole? Stop digging."

Earlier I referred to people who are at the red line of life. They are barely making it from paycheck to paycheck. The following "Take Control of Your Cash Flow" formula from *Rich Dad's CASHFLOW Quadrant* and the following tips are designed to help you take those drastic steps that will help you "stop digging" and start a plan for a better financial future.

What's Next?

Okay, you've decided to discipline yourself and take control of your cash flow. Here is the next step:

- **Follow the "Take Control of Your Cash Flow" formula from *Rich Dad's CASHFLOW Quadrant*.**

Take Control of Your Cash Flow

1. Review your financial statement that you just created.

2. Determine which quadrant of the CASHFLOW Quadrant you receive your income from today.

3. Determine which quadrant you want to receive the bulk of your income from in five years.

4. Begin your cash-flow management plan:

   - Pay yourself first. Put aside a set percentage from each paycheck or each payment you receive from other sources. Deposit that money into an investment savings account. Once your money goes into the account, DO NOT take it out until you are ready to invest it. Congratulate yourself! You have just started managing your cash flow.

   - Focus on reducing your personal debt.

The following are some simple and easy-to-apply tips for reducing and eliminating your personal debt:

Tip #1: If you have credit cards with outstanding balances, keep only one or two credit cards in your wallet.
Keep the other cards out of sight, preferably in a safe or a safety-deposit box.

Any new charges you add to the one or two cards you now have must be paid off every month. Do not incur any further long-term bad debt.

Tip #2: Come up with $150 to $200 extra per month.
Now that you are becoming more and more financially literate, this should be relatively easy to do. If you cannot generate

an additional $150 to $200 per month, then your chances for achieving financial freedom may only be a pipe dream.

Tip #3: Apply the additional $150 to $200 to your monthly payment of ONLY ONE of your credit cards.
You will now pay the minimum PLUS the $150 to $200 on that one credit card.

Pay only the minimum amount due on all other credit cards. Often people try to pay a little extra each month on all their cards, but those cards surprisingly never get paid off.

Tip #4: Once the first card is paid off, apply the total amount you were paying each month on that card to your next credit card.
You are now paying the minimum amount due on the second card PLUS the total monthly payment you were paying on your first credit card.

Continue this process with all your credit cards and other consumer credit such as store charges. With each debt you pay off, add the full amount you were paying on that paid-off debt to the minimum payment of your next debt. As you pay off each debt, the monthly amount you are paying on the next debt will increase.

Tip #5: Once all your credit cards and other bad debt are paid off, continue the procedure with your car and house payments.
If you follow this procedure, you will be amazed at the shortened amount of time it takes for you to be completely debt-free. Most people can be debt-free within five to seven years.

Tip #6: Now that you are completely debt-free, take the monthly amount you were paying on your last debt and put that money toward investments.
Build your asset column.

That's how simple it is.

Other Tips to Help You Get Control

- Start paying all your bills on time to avoid any late fees.

- Find a credit card with a lower interest rate and no annual or transfer fees. Then you may want to consider consolidating your other credit-card debts to that one card. This will allow you to pay less in interest and fees.

- Stop using automated teller machines (ATMs) that charge a fee. That's like paying to use your own money!

You May Need to Get a Grip on Your Spending Habits

- Get in the habit of paying cash. Use a charge card only for emergencies.

- Learn to stop buying on impulse. Use your willpower to say no!

- Shop at wholesale clubs and discount department stores.

- Respect your budget! If you've reached the $200 food limit, skip the potato chips and ice cream.

- Buy generic medicines or find a discount pharmacy.

- Start looking for a part-time business or other way to earn a little more income.

- Turn your thermostat down. Turn off a few lights to save on your electric bill.

- Learn how to winterize your home from top to bottom. Insulate pipes. Get rid of drafty windows. Eliminate those areas where you lose energy.

- Cut back on your home telephone as well as cell-phone usage. This is an area where many people overlook how they can save money.

- Check on your insurance policies. See if you can find some comparable policies for the same cost. Raise your deductible to lower your monthly bills.

In short, start getting in the habit of watching how you spend a dollar here and a dollar there. Give yourself a week and just check on how much you can save by not buying the expensive shampoo or not going out to dinner. Let's say you save $30 or $40 a week. Over a month, that comes to more than $100. Over a year, you're saving $1,200 or more—and that's a nice chunk of change to put towards paying off your credit cards.

Your goal should be to get out of bad debt as quickly as possible so you can start looking to a better future and thinking like the rich. Then you can start buying or building assets that will generate the passive income to pay for your phone bills, electric bills, insurance policies, and more. That is the Rich Dad philosophy of expanding your means to live the lifestyle you choose.

Secured vs. Unsecured Debt

There are two types of debt. *Secured* debt is debt that has collateral backing it up. Typical examples would include a home mortgage or a car loan. *Unsecured* debt is debt without any collateral backing it up. That usually includes credit-card bills, personal loans, and medical bills.

The very first debt to try to get rid of is the unsecured kind. In the Rich Dad system, unsecured debt is most definitely what we call bad debt, and the sooner you can eliminate it, the more in control of your finances you will be. That means paying down your credit cards as quickly as you can, along with any other outstanding debts you may have.

Let's look at credit cards for a moment. No question that they are a wonderful convenience. And there really is no reason to cut them up, as long as you fully understand how they can lead to real financial concerns. For example, many credit cards charge you an annual fee just to have the card. Then, on top of that yearly fee, they of course charge an annual percentage rate (APR) on any monies you owe them.

Take a look at your credit cards. Some charge as high as 20 percent or 25 percent. You'll spend a fortune trying to pay off credit-card debt if you only pay the monthly minimum fee. Get in the habit now of paying off new purchases on your credit card each month.

Let's Focus on Getting Rid of Bad Debt

Here's the precise method I suggest for regaining control of your monthly cash flow:

1. Take all of your credit cards out of your wallet or purse. Following the formula for "Take Control of Your Cash Flow," check the various outstanding balances on each one.

2. Take the cards with the smallest amount of bad debt on them, and pay them in full first.

3. Once you have paid off those cards, put them out of sight. Or, if you don't have the discipline to stop accumulating bad debt with your cards, call up the credit-card company and cancel them.

4. Do the same on the remaining cards. Keep whittling away that outstanding bad debt until it's gone.

Please understand that this is a process that, in most cases, cannot be accomplished in just one or two months. Depending on how much cash you have, this process of whittling down your credit-card debt may take several months, or even years. But do it, because it's a wonderful feeling when you are no longer a slave to those monthly bills.

Once you have control of your credit cards, you may want to take the extra money you have and start to pay off the mortgage on your home. Most homeowners have the option of prepaying their mortgage. In many cases, it makes sense for homeowners to save thousands of dollars by prepaying their mortgage each month. Even just tacking on an extra $50 a month to your principal payment will take years and thousands of dollars off your home mortgage. (Be sure you let the lender know that the additional money is to be added to the *principal* on your mortgage payment.)

The best news is that those individuals who have the willpower to follow these simple measures will find themselves financially solid and free of major bad debt within a few years. It may sound impossible to you in your current financial situation, but trust me—these measures will work for you.

CHAPTER SIX

WHAT IS THE
PRICE OF CHANGE?

---

*"Insanity is doing the same thing over and over again
and expecting different results."*
— *Anonymous*

When I talk on the subject of good debt and bad debt, I often hear questions like the following:

- What if the market crashes?
- What if I make a mistake?
- What if I cannot pay off the debt?
- What if I am not interested in real estate?
- How can I afford to buy real estate when the prices are so high where I live?
- Isn't all debt risky?
- Isn't it better to be debt free?

These are all legitimate questions based on real-world concerns and are not to be taken lightly. I heard one well-known investor say, "Treat all investments as bad investments." But you may also notice what the noted investor did *not* say, "Your concerns are valid, so don't do anything." Yet for millions of people, these fears paralyze them and cause them to do nothing. It is the fear of the unknown that often causes people not to change.

Look one more time at the statistics from the government study. At age 65:

1%   were wealthy

4%   were well off

5%   were still working because they had to

54% were living on family or government support

36% were dead

It's apparent to me that one of the reasons that only 1 out of 100 achieved great wealth is because most people were not able to change when they needed to change. They kept on doing the same thing. I am sure many wanted to change but were paralyzed by fears and doubts such as, "What if the market crashes?" or "What if I make a mistake?" or "What if I cannot pay off the debt?" In other words, many people cannot change because they become prisoners of their own doubts and fears. Their doubts and fears force them to keep doing the same old things, hoping to get a different result, which is the popular definition of insanity.

Newton's Other Law

Rich dad often said, "For people who are afraid of making mistakes, it is often easier to do nothing or to keep doing the same thing." Another of Sir Isaac Newton's universal laws, the Law of Conservation of Energy, states, "A body at rest stays at rest. And a body in motion stays in motion." In other words, a person often finds it easier to remain doing the same thing because a body in motion just stays in motion doing the same thing. And a person finds it difficult to change because it is often difficult to get something new started, because a body at rest stays at rest.

So the price of becoming rich often means doing something different—starting from scratch, getting a new ball rolling, making a few mistakes, and eventually becoming smart at something new. It sounds simple, and it is simple. But the reason most people do not do something simple that could make them rich is found in this law of Newton's.

Change More Than Your Job

In my second book, *Rich Dad's CASHFLOW Quadrant*, I wrote about the four different types of people found in the world of money and business. The diagram below is the CASHFLOW Quadrant.

The four letters stand for: Employee, Self-employed or Small business owner, Big business owner, and Investor. The book goes into the core differences between each of the four people found in each quadrant and what changes people need to make if they want to change quadrants. The reason I bring the CASHFLOW Quadrant up at this time is because, while many people want to change, many more become trapped in their one quadrant. For example, many people leave school, get a job, and remain in the E quadrant until they retire, although they may long to burst out and do something different, such as invest or start their own business.

Many people, even when they make a change, often stay inside the quadrant they are in. For example, many people make changes only inside the E quadrant, which is why they go from job to job looking for more pay or happiness. The reason so few people become wealthy from the E quadrant is because the tax laws are the hardest in that quadrant.

If a person does move from one quadrant to another, the most popular change is from the E quadrant to the S quadrant. A person making this change often says, "I want to do my own thing," or "I want to be my own boss." This is also a difficult quadrant to become wealthy in because, if the person stops working, the income stops coming in. The tax laws are also very tough on the self-employed.

The B and I quadrants are the easiest to achieve great wealth in, but they also pose different personal challenges.

If you would like further distinctions or information on the four different quadrants and how to make the necessary changes, you may want to read *Rich Dad's CASHFLOW Quadrant*.

My advice is to keep your daytime job and give yourself at least five years to start something new in a new quadrant.

To Improve Your Chances of Becoming Rich, Change Quadrants

The reason so many people play the lottery or game shows in the hopes of getting rich is because most people are either in the E or the S quadrant. Most people who do find great wealth are primarily in the B and I quadrants. One of the ways a person can improve their chances of becoming rich is by changing quadrants. There are no guarantees, but at least your chances improve greatly if you operate from the B or I quadrant.

It is estimated that less than 1 percent of the people who achieve great wealth come from either the E or S quadrant. In other words, if you are serious about becoming rich in as short a time as possible, you may need to make a change in quadrants. I know that for me, personally, my chances for achieving great wealth would have been slim to none in either the E or S quadrant. I knew my chances were best in the B and I quadrants, and that is where I made my millions.

When I ask people, "Who *really* wants to be rich?" I also ask if they are willing to change quadrants. Some are. Most are not. Why? The answer is again found in the word "change." For many people, the change required to move from the E and S quadrants on the left side to the B and I quadrants on the right side is too high a price—a price greater than most are willing to pay. For people unwilling to make that change, it is best to find other ways to become rich, such as:

- being cheap and cutting up your credit cards,
- marrying someone for their money, or
- being a crook.

But for those who are willing to consider making the change, I offer the following diagram as a helpful guide to you who are brave of heart—because that is what it often takes, a very brave heart.

The Learning Pyramid

I developed the following diagram in order to explain why simple book knowledge or classroom knowledge is not enough for total financial success. I will use it as a guide to explain what changes a person may need to make in order to become a financially richer person. I call this model *The Learning Pyramid*.

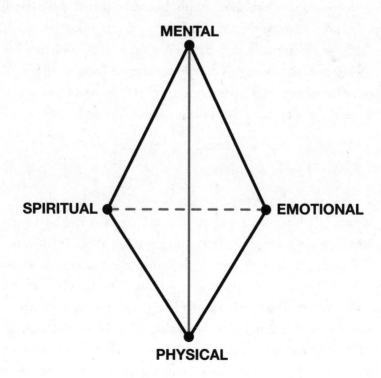

If you have read my third book, *Rich Dad's Guide to Investing*, you may recognize this structure as a tetrahedron, which means a structure with four sides and four points. Some people call it a pyramid. One of my teachers, Dr. R. Buckminster Fuller, said the tetrahedron was one of the most stable structures in the universe, which would explain why the pyramids in Egypt have lasted so long. Regardless, this tetrahedron is useful in explaining the price to make the necessary changes to become rich—or to make any change, for that matter. It also explains why it is so hard for many people to make the necessary changes.

One of my favorite quotes from Albert Einstein goes, "Great spirits have often encountered violent opposition from mediocre minds." I use this statement, not to condemn those who disagree with my ideas, but to remind myself that I have both a great spirit and a mediocre mind.

To explain how the Learning Pyramid works, I'll use the following example. Let's say a person reads a book, and the book says to go out and buy real estate or go find some good debt. So mentally they get the idea, "Go invest in real estate, acquire some good debt, and get rich," which is not a tough thing to do, but most people fail to do it. They may think about it mentally, but fail to do anything physically. Why? Because emotionally they have a problem. The problem arises when their emotional thoughts overpower their mental thoughts. When emotional thoughts are provoked by new mental ideas, we begin to hear the questions listed earlier, questions such as:

- What if the market crashes?
- What if I make a mistake?

These are examples of the emotion of fear rising up to challenge the new mental idea, even a simple idea such as, "Go and buy some real estate, acquire some good debt, and get rich." If the *emotional* thought is stronger than the *mental* thought, then the *physical* result is often no action at all. A person may go into what is called "analysis paralysis" and spend hours physically doing nothing but arguing internally with their thoughts and emotions. Or the person may do as the radio host did during my interview—invalidate the entire idea of investing in real estate. You may recall the radio interviewer saying to me, "I don't want to fix toilets and receive phone calls late at night from tenants."

This is another example of emotional thinking overpowering a new mental idea. The radio host never gave the new idea a chance, thus shutting himself off from the possibility of achieving great wealth and financial freedom. On top of that, toward the end of the interview, he said, "I thought you were going to tell us how to become rich." I replied, "I did. I told you that the way many people become rich and financially free is by having lots of good debt. But all you can think of is toilets." Needless to say, I have not been invited back on his program.

The Power of Ideas

The radio host was not the only person who blocked out ideas that could change his life. I do it. We all do. We all do things that make us successful, and we all do things that keep us unsuccessful. So how do we change when we know we need to change?

My rich dad said, "One of the main reasons most people do not achieve great wealth and financial freedom is simply because *they are afraid of making mistakes.*" He went on to say, "The reason so many smart and well-educated people do not achieve great wealth is because in school they were taught that mistakes are bad. In the real world, the person who makes the most mistakes and learns from them—without lying, cheating, denying, or blaming—wins."

So when you look at the diagram of the Learning Pyramid, one big reason people do not become rich, even though they mentally want to, is because emotionally they have learned to fear making a mistake. Rich dad often said, "It is the fear of failing that causes most people to fail." The fear of failing is an emotional idea that needs to change because that emotional idea often has more power than the mental idea. That is why so few people become rich.

What Worked in School May Not Work in Real Life

When my rich dad said to me years ago, "My banker has never asked me for my report card," one of the most important lessons I learned was that what worked in school may not work in real life. When I meet people who are struggling financially, I often find they're doing so simply because they can't break free from old ideas from family, friends, and school. In other words, they follow ideas they may not even know they are following—ideas such as "don't make mistakes" or "get a safe, secure job" or "work hard, save money, and stay out of debt." These are good ideas for people who cherish security over financial freedom. But they are bad ideas if you are a person who wants to become rich as quickly as possible. So the price of becoming rich is, for many people, the price of examining their old ideas and finding out which ideas need to be changed. But remember, when one mental idea changes, it often requires changing emotionally, physically, and spiritually.

What Worked in War May Not Work in Peace

For me, the fear of failing was not as much of an issue as it is for many people. Failing in school at age 15 because I could not write was one of the best things that happened to me. Today I make more money as a writer than most of the students who were "A" students in English. From that failure, I also learned that my real report card was my financial statement. So for me, I knew that failing was a good thing if I would learn the lessons from the mistakes or failure. I realized I could gain a great advantage by being willing to make more mistakes than people who are academically smarter than I am. The problem was that, while I learned a lot by making mistakes, my impulsive risk-taking and fearless attitude towards failure also limited how much I could learn.

One of the reasons I volunteered to fight in Vietnam was because of the emotional and physical challenges going to war offered. While most people were saying, "I don't want to go to war," or "I'm against the war," I decided it was best to go. So I volunteered, in spite of the fact that I was draft-exempt. The good news was that the Marine Corps did an excellent job of training young men and women to overcome their emotional and physical doubts and limitations. We were trained rigorously to operate with cool mental thought even though we were emotionally terrified and physically challenged. We were trained to get the job done and fulfill the mission, even at the cost of our own lives. That mental, emotional, physical, and spiritual training is what kept me alive in Vietnam.

The bad news was that that training was killing me when I came back from war. I have spent more than 25 years since the war ended trying to *unlearn* what I *learned* in preparation for war.

To survive in war, we were trained to fight in a split second. We often had to shoot before thinking, enter into terrible situations without regard for our own lives, and do horrible things even though we did not want to do them. In other words, we had to physically do things that we may not have wanted to do, and we had to not let our mental thoughts and emotional feelings get in the way of doing our job.

When I returned from war, I discovered that my ability to overcome my fear and my willingness to fight were holding me back. In peacetime, there is no need for a warrior's behavior. I soon realized that there is a big difference between a wartime Marine and a peacetime Marine. People who become generals in the military are those who can be good in peace as well as in war. In peacetime, I needed to learn to think and act more like a politician or a diplomat, even in the Marine Corps. I had to learn to be more patient, to think more before acting, to be kinder, less blunt, and less willing to fight at the drop of a hat. These are lessons I still struggle to learn. I realize that today I would be much more successful—financially, socially, and professionally—if I had made the changes faster, but I was not able to. As I said, I spent 25 years learning to fight, and then I had to spend more than 25 years learning how *not* to fight.

The good news for me is that my ability to override my fear of failure made me a good entrepreneur and investor. But those same abilities also became a limitation to my growth and success. As I wrote earlier, one of Newton's laws states, "For every action, there is an equal and opposite reaction." I needed to make serious personal changes if I wanted my success to grow. For me, my willingness to fight was causing me to win small battles, but I was losing the war. I soon realized that if I didn't make those changes, my success would be limited—just as limited as someone who was afraid of making mistakes. In order to grow, I needed to change.

Every coin has two sides, and every gambler also needs to be a banker. In my life, I had developed my warrior side for 25 years. Since then, I have been developing my diplomatic side. By having both sides, my success has grown. If I had only one side of the coin, I am certain my success would have been greatly limited. In other words, my strengths had become my weaknesses. In order to be whole and complete, I needed to transform my weaknesses into strengths.

Life Is About Change

When people ask me, "What should I invest in?" or "What would you advise me to do?" or "Would you give me the right answer?" I hesitate and diplomatically back away from handing out my answers. The reason I do not like giving out answers is because right answers only work in school and on game shows. In real life, each of us comes with certain strengths, geniuses, and abilities. We also come with weaknesses and, as you may have noticed, often our strengths are also our weaknesses.

To me, life is about change. If you are not changing today, you may be in grave peril because the world is changing faster than ever before. The people who are in the most trouble are those who cling to old right answers and old report cards. With the Internet expanding its reach, the gap between the haves and have-nots will only increase. Today we have kids who are not yet out of high school who are making millions of dollars on the Web. They have not yet had a job and may never have to look for one.

The idea of a job is an idea born out of the Industrial Age. Anyone clinging to old Industrial-Age rules will financially fall behind those who adjust to the new rules of the Information Age—and believe me, the rules are different. If you are clinging to the idea of job security, automatic pay raises, and seniority, you are clinging to rules created in the Industrial Age. The good news is that there has never been more opportunity to gain tremendous wealth. But to gain that wealth, the price is that you may have to change.

The Power of Your Spirit

The uncertainty of change is often frightening. I am as apprehensive of the unknown as anyone else. I have the same self-doubts as anyone else. I hate being wrong and making mistakes as much as anyone else. But the good news is that everyone has to change today. Due to the Internet, change is now democratic. Everyone has to change or pay the price of falling behind, slowly but surely. The good news is that we all have the power to get through this change if we want to access that power. That power is found in the Learning Pyramid. And that power is the power of your spirit.

One of the best things about going to Vietnam was that I witnessed the power of spirit firsthand. If you talk to most veterans who saw actual combat, I am sure most will tell you of individuals who went far beyond the mental, physical, and emotional limitations that hinder most of us in day-to-day life.

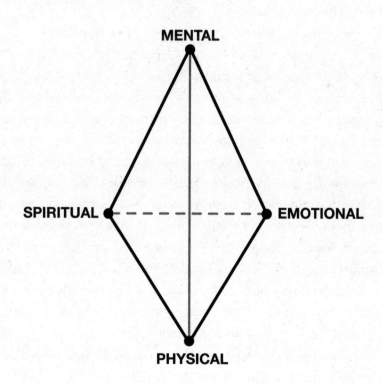

One of my classmates and dear friends from elementary school, Wayne, is a person who spent a year performing one of the most dangerous missions of the war as an LRRP, which stands for Long-Range Reconnaissance Patrol. A "lurp," as the acronym is often pronounced, is a person who is dropped behind enemy lines in a small fighting team to gather information. They often stay behind enemy lines, living off the land, for a week to two months.

One night, I was at Wayne's house in Hawaii discussing the changes we went through from growing up in Hawaii, going to college, and then going to war. We talked about how the experience of war dramatically changed who we are and what our core values are. We both quietly shared stories and spoke in awe of young men who performed feats of courage and heroism far beyond the so-called line of duty.

During this late evening conversation, Wayne quietly said, "There were two missions where I was the only one to come back alive. I am alive today because dead men kept fighting."

I suspect that the reason so many Vietnam veterans have difficulties emotionally is because we fought in a war that we, as a country, did not intend to win. And those who came back are alive only because we had friends give their lives so that we could live. On top of that, we came back to a country that often spit on returning soldiers instead of thanking them for what they did, right or wrong. I too saw dead men who kept fighting—men who physically, mentally, and emotionally were technically dead—yet their spirits kept fighting on, so others could live. As tragic as such experiences are, the lessons learned about the power of the human spirit have been priceless in my life and in Wayne's. Today when I hear someone say, "But what if I lose some money?" or "What if I make a mistake?" or "What if I fail?" I just sort of smile my diplomatic smile, nod my head, and walk away. It is still difficult for me to feel empathy for someone who is afraid of losing $10,000 when I saw others lose their lives.

We do not, however, have to go to war to find examples of the power of the human spirit, a spirit that we all possess. A few years ago

I went to a track meet for physically challenged people. There I saw another classmate who was injured in a car accident and had to have both of his legs amputated. Here he was, 50 years old, both legs gone, and he was running the 100-yard dash on his new prostheses. As he ran, I did not see his physical limitations. All I could see and feel was his spirit driving him. As he ran, his spirit and the spirit of the others who were physically challenged filled the stand of spectators. Most of us began to cry as their spirits touched ours. I was reminded again of the power of the human spirit. I realized that although I was better off physically than he was, he was in far better physical condition than I was. His spirit had turned his physical handicap into a physical, mental, and emotional strength. We all have access to the power of that same spirit.

We All Have Strengths and We All Have Weaknesses

I was not blessed academically. I am not what the school system would call a smart student. I was not blessed emotionally, simply because of my hot temper, lack of patience, and lack of attention to detail. I was also not blessed physically. I am not a great athlete nor was I blessed with great physical beauty. Yet today I would say I have found personal happiness and financial freedom because I was always reminded of the power of the human spirit. Both my dads, as well as my mom, had that spirit and encouraged me to call on that power in times of great personal doubt. I am alive today because, as my classmate Wayne said, "Dead men kept fighting." I am who I am today because I married a woman who has a strong, powerful spirit—a spirit that trusted me and stood beside me when others said she should leave.

If not for Kim's spiritual strength, I know I would not be where I am today. I would not be here today if not for my friends who stood by me and helped me up when I fell and lost faith in myself. I have attained financial freedom not because of my physical, emotional, or mental strength. I was encouraged by those around me to go on, even when I lost touch with my own spirit. I was able to make changes and grow to meet new challenges simply because other spirits inspired my spirit to carry on. And for me, I have always found freedom when I found my spirit.

In times of deep personal doubt and darkness, I often reflect on a poem written by Ella Wheeler Wilcox which I read in James Allen's book, *As a Man Thinketh.*

> You will be what you will to be;
> Let failure find its false content
> In that poor word "environment,"
> But spirit scorns it, and is free.
>
> It masters time, it conquers space;
> It cows that boastful trickster, Chance,
> And bids the tyrant Circumstance,
> Uncrown, and fill a servant's place.
>
> The human Will, that force unseen,
> The offspring of a deathless Soul,
> Can hew a way to any goal,
> Though walls of granite intervene.
>
> Be not impatient in delay,
> But wait as one who understands;
> When spirit rises and commands,
> The gods are ready to obey.

It was because of my spirit that I was able to learn mentally, to harness my emotions properly, to take physical action—even though filled with doubt, to fall down, and to stand back up.

WHAT IS THE PRICE OF FIXING YOUR FINANCIAL REPORT CARD?

"Accounting leads to accountability."
– Rich dad

I often hear, "I don't want to learn about accounting. I'm not interested in keeping an updated financial statement." When I hear comments such as these, I agree that it is a person's individual choice to learn what they choose to learn. At that point I often repeat a saying from rich dad, "Accounting leads to accountability." In other words, one of the benefits of studying accounting and continually striving to improve your financial statements is that the process improves your accountability to yourself. And being accountable to yourself is the price you need to pay if you really want to become rich.

After I lost my first business, rich dad said to me, "When your car is broken, you take it to trained professional mechanics and they fix your car. The problem with your financial problems is that only one person can fix those problems, and that person is you." Explaining further, he said, "Your financial situation is much like your golf game. You can read books, attend seminars, hire a coach, and take lessons, but ultimately, only you can improve your golf game." One of the reasons so few people attain great wealth is because, when people get into financial trouble, they do not know how to get out of trouble. No one has ever taught them the basics of how to diagnose the particular financial problem they may be in. As a result, although people may know they are in financial trouble, they do not know how to read a financial statement or how to keep accurate financial records, so they do not know how serious their financial problems are or how to fix them.

Facing my ruined financial statement was a painful experience. Yet facing my problems was the best thing I could have done. Rather than wasting time pretending I had no problems, I faced my financial statement and my problems and found out exactly what I did not know, as well as what I needed to learn in order to fix my financial situation.

Watching me groan and moan as I faced the financial train wreck, rich dad said, "If you are willing to face the truth and learn from your mistakes, you will learn far more about money than I could ever teach you." He went on to explain, saying, "When you face your own personal financial statement, you face yourself and your own financial challenges. You begin to find out what you know and what you do not know. When you look at your financial statement, you become accountable to yourself. Just as a golfer cannot blame anyone else for their bad scorecard, once you look at your accounting records, you become personably accountable."

Facing my financial problems and solving them was the best education I could have received because, by facing my mistakes, I became accountable for my own shortcomings. By facing my financial statement, I found out that I had failing financial grades. I realized that I was not as financially smart as I thought I was. By improving those grades, I learned what I needed to learn in order to become financially free—and that is the price I paid.

A Final Thought

There are many ways to become rich. One way is to cut up your credit cards and live cheaply. I chose not to do that because the price was too high. Another way is to marry someone for his or her money. And again, I could have done that, but the price was way too high, although it is a popular way to get rich quickly. Another way is to get rich by being a crook, but to me, that price is definitely too high. And another way to become rich is to improve your financial literacy, your financial intelligence, and be accountable to yourself—accountable for your results, your continuing education, and your personal development in becoming a better human being. To me, that was a price I was willing to pay.

Take one more look at a financial statement as a reminder of what my rich dad pointed out as important.

Summary of What's Important for Financial Intelligence

Thank you for reading this book. I hope that you will pay the price to learn what you need to learn in order to become financially free.

Profession _____ *Player* _____

Goal: Get out of the Rat Race and onto the Fast Track by building up your **Passive Income** to be **greater** than your **Total Expenses**

INCOME STATEMENT

INCOME

Description	Cash Flow
Salary:	
Interest/Dividends:	
Real Estate/Business:	

Auditor _____
(Person on your right)

Passive Income : $ _____
(Cash Flow from Interest/Dividends + Real Estate/Business)

Total Income: $ _____

EXPENSES

Taxes:	
Home Mortgage Payment:	
School Loan Payment:	
Car Loan Payment:	
Credit Card Payment:	
Retail Payment:	
Other Expenses:	
Child Expenses:	
Loan Payment:	

Number of Children: _____
(Begin game with 0 Children)
Per Child Expense: $ _____

Total Expenses: $ _____

BALANCE SHEET

Monthly Cash Flow (PAYCHECK): $ _____
(Total Income - Total Expenses)

ASSETS

Savings:		
Stocks/Funds/CDs:	# of Shares:	Cost/Share:
Real Estate/Business:	Down Pay:	Cost:

LIABILITIES

Home Mortgage:	
School Loans:	
Car Loans:	
Credit Cards:	
Retail Debt:	
Real Estate/Business:	Mortgage/Liability:
Loan:	

G101CT8Lv2

Robert T. Kiyosaki

Robert T. Kiyosaki, Best known as the author of *Rich Dad Poor Dad*— the #1 personal finance book of all time—Robert Kiyosaki has challenged and changed the way tens of millions of people around the world think about money. He is an entrepreneur, educator and investor who believes the world needs more entrepreneurs. With perspectives on money and investing that often contradict conventional wisdom, Robert has earned a reputation for straight talk, irreverence and courage.

Notes

UNFAIR advantage
THE POWER OF FINANCIAL EDUCATION

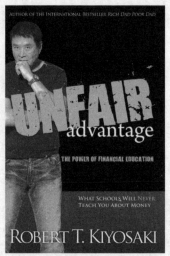

If there is any financial education, the courses are taught by financial planners and bankers... the agents of Wall Street and the big banks, the very people that caused and profited from the financial crisis. This book is about real financial education.

This book is about the five unfair advantages a real financial education offers:

- The Unfair Advantage of Knowledge
- The Unfair Advantage of Taxes
- The Unfair Advantage of Debt
- The Unfair Advantage of Risk
- The Unfair Advantage of Compensation

On the heels of his 2010 *New York Times* best-seller *Conspiracy of the Rich,* Robert Kiyosaki takes a new and hard-hitting look at the factors that impact people from all walks of life as they struggle to cope with change and challenges that impact their financial world.

In *Unfair Advantage – The Power of Financial Education* Robert challenges readers to change their context and act in a new way. Readers are advised to stop blindly accepting that they are 'disadvantaged' people with limited options. They are encouraged to act beyond their concept of limited options and challenge the preconception that they will struggle financially all of their lives.

Robert's fresh approach to his time-tested messages includes clear, actionable steps that any individual or family can take, starting with education. Education becomes applied knowledge, a powerful tactic with measurable results.

In true Rich Dad style, readers will be challenged to understand two points of view, and experience how financial knowledge is their unfair advantage.

Order your copy at
richdad.com today!

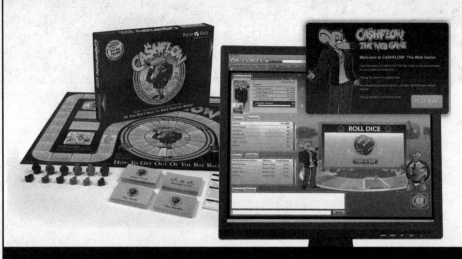

The Board Game *USA Today* Calls Monopoly® on Steroids!

Leading researchers teach that we only retain 10% of what we read, but 90% of what we experience.

CASHFLOW 101, developed by Robert Kiyosaki, author of the #1 personal-finance book of all time, **Rich Dad Poor Dad,** is an educational board game that simulates real-life financial strategies and creates an experience that teaches you how to get out of the Rat Race and onto the Fast Track by making your money work for you—not the other way around.

Robert Kiyosaki
Investor, Entrepreneur,
Educator and Author

- Practice real-world investing with play money.
- Learn the differences between an asset and a liability.
- Discover the power of understanding your personal financial statement.

Now you can play the *CASHFLOW* game online for FREE!

Rich Dad knows that online game play connects people in a most engaging way. Now, *CASHFLOW The Web Game* is live online and ready for you to play with others around the world. No software is required. Register in the Rich Dad community and play right from your internet browser. Visit richdad.com and click on the *CASHFLOW* game link.

Order your copy at
richdad.com today!

RICH ◆ DAD